C000285963

George Murray, a Schoolteacher

for St Kilda 1886-87

George Murray, a Schoolteacher for St Kilda 1886-87

Maureen Kerr

The Islands Book Trust

Published in 2013 by The Islands Book Trust

www.theislandsbooktrust.com

Copyright remains with the named author. Other than brief extracts for the purpose of review, no part of this publication may be reproduced in any form without the written consent of the publisher and copyright owner.

© The Islands Book Trust 2013

ISBN: 978-1-907443-55-8

Text © Maureen Kerr
Line drawings and paintings © Maureen Kerr

All rights reserved. No part of this publication may be reproduced, stored in a retrieval system, or transmitted in any other form or by any means, electronic, mechanical, photocopying, recording or otherwise without the prior written permission of the publishers. This book may not be lent, hired out, resold or otherwise disposed of by way of trade in any form of binding or cover other than that in which it is published, without the prior consent of the publishers.

The author and publisher would like to thank the Murray family for permission to reproduce extracts from the North Uist diary and family photographs. In addition the publisher would like to thank Donnie Morrison for his work in restoring the photographs prior to publication.

The Islands Book Trust, Ravenspoint Centre, Kershader, South Lochs, Isle of Lewis, HS2 9QA. Tel: 01851 880737

Typeset by Erica Schwarz (www.schwarz-editorial.co.uk)
Cover design by Raspberry Creative Type
Printed and bound by Martins the Printers, Berwick upon Tweed

Contents

Introduction

THE STREET - ST. KILDA.

CLEIT WITH FLAG IRIS
ABOVE FEATHER STORE
JUNE '05

MUCH has been written about St Kilda. Some might say too much and most of it not by the islanders themselves. A lot of information has been gleaned from the people who went out to work there; the diaries and accounts of ministers of the church, factors and nurses and of course, the school teachers sent out in a more or less continuous stream from the mid-1800s until the island's evacuation in 1930. This book is about one of those teachers; George Murray, who was sent out to St Kilda in 1886 until 1887.

I thought I knew quite a bit about George Murray. He has been widely quoted and discussed in many of the informative books published about St Kilda. In one, he has a whole chapter to himself and most of the information has come from a diary he kept while out there on the island.

About six years ago, I was given a copy of the transcription of this diary. With the transcription was a letter dated 1947 from George's son Iain (John), a headmaster in Portree High School. It was clear from this letter that he had lent the diary to the eminent naturalist James Fisher, for him to make a copy of it, to ascertain if there was anything in the diary about the wildlife on St Kilda. James had the diary transcribed (returning the original to Iain) and on his death, amongst a mass of scientific and other papers, this transcription came to light and was, we think, then given to the National Library, a copy also being lodged with the National Trust for Scotland.

My first reading of this transcription left a profound impression. I found it utterly fascinating, resonating with George's personality and the islanders' lifestyle at that time. I wanted to know more about him. From his diary I discovered his home had been in Rogart in Sutherland, a place I knew very well indeed, having lived in the area for many years and in conversation about a year or two later with a local Rogart historian, I asked him if he knew who George Murray was, mentioning the diary I'd come across.

'Oh aye' was the reply, 'He was from hereabouts right enough and ended up a Free Church minister down round about Nairn somewhere. I mind hearing a window fell on him and he died.' Taken aback by this revelation, I asked about the accident. No, he couldn't say what had happened or where, just that he'd heard that a window had fallen on him. He supposed there was immediate family still living round about. It filled me with curiosity and I decided I would like to know even more about George Murray.

After a lot of research and even more dead ends, as the area is inundated with Murrays, I found the family I was looking for; one of them still living on the family farm of Davochbeg in Rogart. Morven Murray, the widow of Alec Murray, a great nephew of George's, was more than helpful in putting me in touch with this particular branch of Murrays. Having finally found them, I was able to ask for permission to use the material available to write about him and I began to find out just what a special man he had been. Instinct had not been wrong; he was worth writing about.

Then there was another surprise in store. On looking over the photocopies of the original handwritten diary, I discovered there were not one, but two diaries. The second was certainly the St Kilda diary, but the first one was the diary he had kept during the summer months while in North Uist as a missionary and teacher, the year before he travelled to St Kilda.

It made very interesting reading and I felt that some of the information it contained had to be included, as it was an historical and cultural account of customs and of the people living in that area of North Uist at that time. It uncovered just what a missionary/teacher's role was like in the 1880s and revealed a lot about George as a young man of twenty-four. There is no doubt also, that this trip to North Uist served him well in what he could expect in terms of comfort and lifestyle on St Kilda.

It helped in the reading of those two diaries to know more about George Murray's history; where he came from, his family background and what he went on to achieve after St Kilda and before his untimely death in 1918, when he was still in his fifties. Therefore the book has been divided up into two sections. The first is a short history of the Murrays, followed by the life story of George and what he went on to become as a minister of the United Free Church of Scotland. To this account some information has been added from the North Uist diary he kept during the summer months at Locheport in 1885. Then, last of all, a full transcription of the more familiar St Kilda diary.

Both diaries begin and end very abruptly, but with research and information available, it is possible to speculate fairly accurately as to what was going on at the time, before and after he started writing. Some of the diary entries are ambiguous and I have inserted notes to help make sense of these, again based on much research. There is also other information and some anecdotes which relate to modern times from my own observations during the ten years I spent out on St Kilda. The diary entries by George himself are in italics.

The diaries stand alone in their simplicity and in those diaries the man shines through. His intelligence, energy, fairness, generosity of spirit and humour are all set in a well determined path for the future, but there is no doubt that St Kilda certainly came as a bit of a shock to him, even after his North Uist experiences, and we see him bewildered and angry, incredulous and in some cases fearful for his safety.

It has been said by others that he was a very naïve and over sensitive young man and while that may appear true in some of the predicaments in which he found himself, his incredible courage should not be ignored. There were heart-stopping moments on sheer cliffs, daring situations on treacherous seas that would have reduced other men to utter panic, but not him. He dealt with them all very courageously and calmly and he also stood up very firmly against the wrath of several bullies on the island, although he makes it quite clear in the diary that he abhors conflict and violence. He genuinely wished to improve his scholars' lot in life and this trait is evident in the way he enthusiastically embarked on his new school in Carinish, North Uist and his obvious delight and satisfaction in his pupils' attainments. He introduced a singing class on St Kilda, which would have been a novel and creative addition to the standard teaching fare on offer and at first met with opposition from the minister, Reverend John MacKay, but quietly steered things around into getting the result he wanted. These patient but persistent qualities stood him in good stead later on in his life.

St Kilda, or rather the main island of Hirta, is roughly about two and a half miles in diameter. It is part of a group of islands and stacks some fifty miles out in the Atlantic, off the coast of the Outer Hebrides and about a hundred miles west of mainland Scotland. Human habitation goes back around several thousand years and for many, St Kilda represents

SOAY LAMB
ST KILDA MAY '08

the epitome of an idyllic community, working together in harmony with nature over that time, but ultimately seduced by the comforts of a modern way of life.

A politician visiting the island for the first time said of it:

> Few who have been there and stood in the deserted village surrounded by the cries of a million sea birds, can fail to be moved by this place and its history. It is a place apart; a place of drama, its inaccessibility amplifying its remoteness, creating a perception of being at the edge of the Western World.

It is unique in that it is the only place in Britain which still retains its natural volcanic features and has not been eroded or worn down by glaciation, unlike most of the mountains in mainland Scotland. Standing on its highest point on Conachair and looking down into Village Bay it is apparent that the hills rising above the ruined crater still have that 'pointyness' that one sees, for example, in some of the volcanic hills in the Caribbean.

St Kilda is owned by the National Trust for Scotland and although there is a military presence it is very carefully managed by the Trust with the support of other agencies; Scottish Natural Heritage, Historic Scotland and the local authority, Comhairle nan Eilean Siar.

It has double World Heritage status, one of only a handful in the world. A small visitor centre on the island, manned in the summer, welcomes more than three thousand visitors a year, quite a staggering number when you consider it is incredibly difficult to get on to; the key deterrent being weather in preventing landings.

The Vikings would have known it intimately as a stopping off point as they swept round northern Scotland in their longships. They would have taken on water there and there is evidence that they may have colonised the islands, as the flock of sheep that roams St Kilda today has its origins in the Norse lands.

In the late 1800s the domestic sheep that were on the main island of Hirta and on Boreray were of the blackface breed, which the St Kildans, although existing primarily on a diet of sea birds, used for wool, milk, mutton and cheese; but on the island of Soay, the hardy brown animals, more goat like than sheep, left behind by the Vikings were still in residence. There did not seem to be much mixing or crossing of the two flocks as far as I am aware, although the St Kildans went to Soay for sheep to kill for eating and presumably their fleece. After the evacuation of the island in 1930, the Marquis of Bute, who aquired ownership of St Kilda, caused in 1932, 107 of the Soay sheep flock of mixed ages and sex, to be tranferred from Soay onto Hirta, the domestic blackface having been gathered and taken off Hirta at the time of the evacuation and subsequently sold at auction in Oban. Some blackface sheep remained on Boreray and the small flock there can still be seen on its precipitous hills and cliffs.

Domestic cows arriving later to the island needed rich grass, a lot of it in the form of hay for winter feed. This crop was precarious in this storm lashed place, even in summer and therefore the cow was not always an affordable luxury. They also needed a bull for calves, thus another mouth to feed for a fragile and already stretched agricultural economy.

On an island surrounded by ocean, there should have been much made of the fishing to supplement their diet, but this was not always possible, exposed as they were to the pounding Atlantic seas.

For the last ten years I have worked out on St Kilda as a chef on the military base, one month on, one month off, flying in and out by helicopter. As an artist and writer I feel deeply privileged to have spent so long out there. I have walked it, written about it, painted it, drawn it and photographed it in all its moods; in howling 120mph gales, in deep pristine snow, high up on the cliff faces and boulder fields and down in the old settlement in Gleànn Mór. It is an artist's paradise with its changing, shifting clear light and dramatic cloud and weather patterns. It has truly been a field trip of a lifetime for me.

During the summers when I was there the base personnel had access to a powerful Polar RIB boat and in the evenings or weekends in good weather we'd go out to lift our lobster pots and maybe take a trip round the island, venturing into some of the many caves at the base of the cliffs. One, on the south side of Dun, is accessed by a narrow fissure penetrating

NORTH FACING CLIFFS
WITH THE TUNNEL - ST. KILDA .

deep into the cliff face. It eventually opens out into an immense cathedral cave of rock with a shingle beach at the far end. It was always full of seals and we'd see them rushing out under the boat, escaping to the sea. We'd inch our way back out, then hurtle off up the coast, through the small stacs between Soay and Hirta, sweeping past Glen Bay and the Tunnel; the latter a vast cavernous geo and a maelstrom of turbulent water, where there were always seals playing and calling and everywhere there were birds – thousands and thousands of them; fulmars, gannets, guillemots, razorbills, kittiwakes, puffins, petrels and shearwaters.

Huge cloud-like drifts of them would rise up from the cliffs as we passed by on our way out to Boreray and the Stacs to the north east of the main island, and once there, great snow carpets of them peeled off the ledges to float and soar screaming around us and the boat, the skies dark with them.

Back we'd come into the safety of Village Bay and the small jetty, me to go back to the cookhouse with anything we'd caught and the guys to clean the boat, sort out the creels and fishing lines, then float the boat round and onto the cradle to be winched up by tractor to the shelter of the base. A trip like that certainly satisfied the soul.

The author, Frank Fraser-Darling, said of islands:

> You can establish a profound personal relationship with
> islands, which calls you back to them again and again. Each is a
> personality rather than a place, for an island is finite, embraced
> by the wind and sea and sky. It is a whole world in miniature,
> yet small enough to give you the feeling that you belong and so
> perfect a model of God's universe, that every hour of every day
> is a season of rare enchantment.

This describes perfectly for me that intimate connection you can have with an island; forever embedded like a little lodestone in your heart, taken out in your mind's eye to be viewed again and again, never to be forgotten.

However, for some, islands can be fearful places of entrapment, anxiety and panic. The feeling of not being able to escape can be overwhelming. For the St Kildans of the past, there was no escape except by the occasional passing ship, but all were very accepting of their tiny homeland, for that is what it was; their home.

Everything has been meticulously researched but as with any endeavour such as this there are bound to be a few errors. Hopefully they are not too drastic and won't detract from the readability of the finished product.

I have many people to thank for encouragement, research and for getting it to the stage it's now at, so here they are, not necessary in order of importance: Alasdair MacRae, friend, fellow musician and genealogist, for all the hard work he put in, researching the Murray family and his patience with my over-enthusiastic approach to it all, as he was dragged off all over the countryside to visit people, churchyard graves and various sites of interest for the book; Alasdair MacEachen for patiently and meticulously reading, correcting the manuscript and giving me information on things I did not know, a massive thank you and to Jean who translated much of the Gaelic for me; the Murray family for all their help, information and encouragement once they'd got over the shock that someone wanted to write about their grandfather, especially Jennifer, Anne, Morven and Christine; my sister Dr Hazel Crichton for her encouragement and support; Morag MacDonald, one of the nurses out on St Kilda, for her support, information and being a good walking buddy out there; Roddy MacLeod for advice on local crofting systems and information about the island; Will Miles for introducing me to the petrels and a life-long love affair with these wee 'fairy birds'; Ali MacDonald, one of my supervisors out on the island to whom nothing was too much trouble to organise and deal with and who went out of his way to help make my life easier out there when the temperatures and tempers in the cookhouse soared and things became fraught; Bill Anderson from Edinburgh who sorted out the

CALUM MÒR'S
HOUSE
ST. KILDA '13

complexities of the Free Church for me; Martin Petrie, whose doorstep I chose at random in Kilninver and who turned out to be the local historian, who knew all about George and the Kilninver church and was so generous with that information; John MacDonald, Rogart who first told me about the window incident and who gave freely, information about the local area; Susan Bain, NTS Inverness, for her information on the manse. I was lucky to be on the island at the time the manse was being stripped back to its original state before being renovated and was able to see just how it would have been during George's time; Katherine Barr, Claddach Kirkibost who looked at my early art attempts of the island and gave me good advice and encouragement (she still does); John MacDonald and his nephew Angus MacNab from Sidinish, Locheport who took me around the area where George was based in 1885 and fed me much information on the community in Locheport, my grateful thanks; the Islands Book Trust, for believing I could (eventually) deliver up a book to them.

Maureen Kerr

Part One

George Murray's Story

THE FACTOR'S HOUSE
AND FEATHER STORE
VILLAGE BAY, ST.KILDA   PAL '13

A HISTORY of the Murray family reveals that there are to all intents
and purposes, two distinct branches of Murrays, although all are
descended from one man, Freskyn de Moravia. In the eighth and ninth
centuries, Caithness and Sutherland remained firmly in Norse control, but
a change occurred in the early tenth century when Alexander (who ruled
most of Scotland at that time), together with his younger brother David
(who became King after Alexander's death in 1124), set about reorganising
the Catholic Church in Scotland and went on to found monasteries and
Bishoprics up and down the country. They also introduced feudalism and
were generous to the Norman knights and barons, giving them land to be
held in feudal service to the crown.

In the year 1130 we hear of Freskyn de Moravia for the first time. He
was a Lowland Pict or Scot, not of Flemish descent as has been suggested
and he was a common ancestor of the great Scottish families of Athol,
Bothwell, Sutherland and probably Douglas.

Freskyn had built a castle on a northern estate near Elgin and had other
extensive lands in Moray, which had been given to him by King David in

addition to southern territories in Linlithgow. We also hear, around this time, of a small branch of the de Moravias (or Murrays), settling north of the River Oykel and in or around 1196 Freskyn's grandson, Hugo, received for family loyalty to the Scottish crown, lands in South Caithness known as Southland or Sutherland, comprising of; Criech, Dornoch, Rogart, Golspie, Clyne, Loth, Lairg and Kildonan. In addition, Hugo also held the Duffus Estate in Moray only thirty miles south of Dunrobin by sea.

In or around 1214, Hugo's son, William, became the first Earl of Sutherland and it is interesting to note that Hugo's tenure of the Estates of Sutherland has been preserved until the present day in the charter room at Dunrobin Castle in Golspie. Of Hugo's three sons (William being the eldest), Walter succeeded to Linlithgow, Duffus and the estates in Moray and eventually these were severed from Sutherland ownership, while his third son, Andrew, became Bishop of Moray; and there, in a nutshell, is a short history of the Murrays and their connection to Sutherland.

George Murray was born at 5.30am on the 2nd of November 1860 at Achnaluachrach near West Langwell, above Rogart in Sutherland. He was the fourth son to be born to John and Jane Murray, who went on to have another three children. George's father John had been a groomsman to the then Duke of Sutherland on Dunrobin Estate and John's father Hugh had also worked on the Estate. In 1854, John aged 26, had married Jane Ross, three years older than himself. Jane was a stonemason's daughter from Rosehall and shortly after their marriage, John took on the tenancies of the small farms of Achnaluachrach and Achtomolinnie.

The clearance of people from Rogart in 1819 by the Duke of Sutherland's factors, to make way for more productive crops such as sheep, had caused many of the remaining farms to begin to revert to nature and no doubt John Murray was keen to instigate improvements on his newly tenanted farm lands, in keeping with the trend of the time towards enthusiastic reclamation of moorland and farmland. Achnaluachrach (the field of the rushes) was, with Achtomolinnie (the field of the small hill with some bits of bog), around two hundred acres, on a high plateau to the west of West Langwell above Rogart and the main Strath far below.

Achnaluachrach was the main farm and had a good farm house of five rooms, farm steadings and fanks and had at the time of his occupation, around 120 acres of arable land. These would have given a reasonable yield of corn and hay and other root crops.

Achtomolinnie, south west of the main farmhouse, was the hirsal, which supported the sheep and rough grazing for the cows. We know from a census of around this time that they also had two servants; this would imply that the farm was well able to support itself and provide for all there. The census ten years later, in 1871, tells us a slightly different story; that the farm had reduced to forty-five acres, of which only twenty of these were arable and cultivated, while the servants had been reduced to one.

Not much is known about the servant, Sackville Murray, who was possibly a distant relation and known to the family as 'Secky' and would have been around nineteen or twenty years old. However, when I went to photograph Achnaluachrach recently, I was to discover that 'Secky's' grand-daughter still lived in the original house, which had been extended and renovated, the original being smaller and thatched.

Jessie Alice gave me great insight into how things were during her childhood, with many stories of the area, who her friends were, where they lived, her daily trips to school and back, just a mile and a half along the road at West Langwell (where George also would have gone), and indeed made Achnaluachrach 'live' for me. Apparently at that time, according to Jessie, there were quite a few 'Seckys' around. It was the custom in the area to sometimes give children the name of the parents' benefactor. It was seen as a mark of respect and the old Duke was a Sackville.

Certainly the surrounding area is delightful. Wide open vistas to the south and east overlooking a large lochan (Loch Pressnaskianach), with small rounded hills to the north and north-west. The whole area is one of fresh openness and freedom with the great wheeling skies above. (It's no wonder that George, while he was in North Uist in 1885, was much upset by the news that the whole family were moving down to Davochbeg and the Strath below and he would never again return to his happy boyhood home.)

In 1873, after a short illness, George's mother died aged just forty-seven and a cousin of John's, Ellen Macintosh, came to look after the housekeeping and general welfare of the family.

John's family were however, growing up, the older boys ready to set out into the wider world. 'Young' John, born a year after they were married, would have been eighteen years, his brothers Hugh, seventeen, Robert, sixteen, George, thirteen, Alexander, ten, and Margaret aged seven. Another daughter Helen had not survived infancy.

It must have been more and more of a struggle, even with some of his sons assisting him, to keep the farm viable with the few acres that were left and accordingly we next hear of them in 1885, having secured the lease of Davochbeg farm from the Duke, a short distance south of Pittentrail and with an eight roomed farmhouse. It is still there and lived in by one of the Murray family today.

In 1881 the farmlands of Davoch, which extended to most of the Strath, had been in the ownership of one George Barclay, a wealthy businessman and amounted to some 2,000 acres, employing eleven men. It was on fertile plains, sheltered and sunny and would have been hugely productive. A few years later it was in the ownership of the Duke, who had it broken up into smaller farms with leases attached.

The Davochbeg farm lease was signed in 1885 by John, who would now be fifty-seven years old. The family moved down almost immediately, in the May of that year, while George was away from home in North Uist. One of John's sons, Alexander, and his wife Georgina were now living with the family and it was he who subsequently took on the running of the farm as John slowly relinquished much of the day to day tasks. George meanwhile, had enrolled in King's College in Aberdeen. He had just finished his second term there and the following year emerged with a degree in Classics, with a view to becoming a Free Church Minister.

The summer of 1885, found him in North Uist as a teacher and missionary at the instigation of 'The Ladies' Association.' There were many philanthropically motivated and charitable organisations at this time and one of these was The Ladies' Association, founded and established in

1850, their main base being in Edinburgh. Their aim was to support the establishment of Free Church schools in the Highlands and Islands as well as the promotion of intellectual and spiritual needs. They also aided Gaelic speaking young men to become students for the ministry. The advantages of being a Gaelic speaker were obvious, as almost all of the population living in the Highlands, especially on the western seaboard, spoke only Gaelic. It is interesting to note however that George was not a native Gaelic speaker. Rogart was just that bit too far east. There were a smattering of native speakers at the time in the district but these dwindled to almost none in successive years. They were an extremely industrious group of ladies and no doubt, during the three years that George attended King's College in Aberdeen, they were very active in recruiting from the students there.

'The Ladies' were also keen on sending these young students out on field work as teachers and missionaries when colleges were closed during the summer; a sort of work experience situation, which of course satisfied their aims, but also satisfied the adventurous spirit and imagination of their students. It had certainly appealed to George, for he had a keen sense of adventure and it would have helped fit him for the public persona he would have on becoming a minister of the Free Church. He was more than eager to fill in the summer months in gaining experience of preaching and of furthering his fluency in the Gaelic language and he set off buoyantly for Locheport from Oban at the end of March on the *Hebridean*, sailing up between Mull and the mainland, revelling in the glorious mountain scenery with its snow clad tops.

The journey seems to have been one of constant island hopping as he went from Mull to Coll, Jura then Rum and then onto a couple of destinations on Skye, where he wrote that he saw for the first time the unusual sight of 'the people carrying on their backs, seaware, which they use as manure for the land'. He had 'MacLeod's Maidens', which were three rocks of an imposing size pointed out to him on the shoreline, '… *the largest resembles a tall stout lady clad from head to heels in a cloak. The other two of similar forms are much less and appear as if they were addressing their superior … A curious spectacle they present indeed …*'

He finally made it from Dunvegan across the Minch to Locheport, arriving at the anchorage in the loch at about half past four in the morning. Two men were there to meet him and they transported him and his baggage in a small boat two miles further up the loch to a small township and his lodging house. Local historian John MacDonald and his nephew, Angus MacNab, pointed out to me a modern house beside a small lochan as being the area where the Ladies' Association at one time had a house or school house, so it's more than likely that this was where he lived. His neighbour, Archibald MacCuish, (his diary definitely says 'Archibald' but John MacDonald thinks that he was in fact an Angus MacCuish) lived just across the road from him, so that his house being on that spot would have made sense. There are the remains of the MacCuish house still to be seen.

The Ladies' Association house was set aside principally for visitors such as himself. The women in the community looked after him, supplying him with food and the community supplied peats for his fire and comfort. The house would also contain basic furniture for his needs. He feels great pity for many of these local people, for although they are extremely kind to him, they appear to live in rough huts with their animals at one end of the house and themselves at the other.

This community was still a very new community. In 1851 the people belonging to thirty-four crofts were evicted from their ancestral homes at

Sollas on the west side of the island. Many of them went to Australia but the rest ended up at Langass, a very small marginal piece of land just to the north west of Locheport. They managed to exist in rough turf huts here for a year before moving across the loch, where they settled down along the coastline, building rough huts and small stone dwellings, all the while tackling the gargantuan task of wresting a living from the incredibly poor soil and bog. They should, in fact, have been praised for their efforts, but to George, used to the better way of life and dwellings in his own crofting area in Rogart; it appeared that they had always lived like this and he felt sorry for them.

He became aware of his shortcomings in the Gaelic language almost immediately after his first prayer meeting the next day and returned later to his house quite depressed and feeling '*very unqualified for the work, owing to my limited knowledge of the language*', but a few days later he met with the minister at Clachan, who was very kind and encouraging and gave him heart to tackle the tasks ahead. I had assumed that the minister at Clachan was a Free Church minister and indeed that was the case. A small thatched Free Church building stood at the cross roads at Clachan; later a new Free Church was built a little further south on a small hillock between 1889–1893.

His life soon became one of endless prayer meetings, visiting families in the area, especially the sick and elderly, setting up a Sabbath school and a school in Claddach Carinish, in order to teach the children there, not only the 'three Rs', but some English as well, which would be useful for them in later life. His house visits also helped him converse more freely in the Gaelic, although it's obvious that he was still a bit frustrated with the speed at which he was progressing. He also found time for study, mostly Gaelic, but managed to pursue some Greek and other fairly weighty works, one imagines, as an alternative diversion!

The end of April saw some very stormy weather and curtailed quite a bit of his visiting. He went to see an old man nearby one evening and was taken aback by the fact that the poor man could not read, never having had any 'learning' and he could not read his Bible to comfort himself in his old age. George returned to his house reflecting on this and it occurred to him just how many privileges he has had himself, which have been denied to others and he resolved that '*to whomsoever much is given, of them shall much be required*'.

A word should also be said at this point about the mileage he was expected to cover; all of it on foot. From his lodging to Clachan, it would be about two and a half miles. The distance from there to Claddach Carinish would be another three miles. The main town of Lochmaddy was nine or ten miles distant and most of it was over bogs, skirting lochans and bleak heather moorland. The time and effort it took to get from one place to another was considerable and he was also at the mercy of whatever weather there was on the day.

He set off one morning across a very wet and rough moor to Claddach Carinish to set up his school for the children. He was given an old 'black house' as his school house and enrolled about twenty children on the first day. The fact that he had no text books did not deter him and he wrote out the alphabet on slates to begin the job in hand.

Eventually he ended up with around thirty pupils and he decided that as all were very keen to learn, he would commit himself to going there twice a week so that essential progress could be made, before the few months he had with them was at an end. He wrote, '*My eyes were terribly sore with the smoke*'. In the old black houses the fire was on a hearth in the centre of the room, the smoke from which, eventually, made its way up through a small hole in the roof above. The room would have been constantly hazy with the blue peat smoke.

Eventually he got text books for them and arranged the pupils into their respective classes on benches. There are a lot of children for him to teach and he was frustrated as he struggled to get through to many of them, some of whom have no way it seems of helping themselves at all, '*As yet they do not much for themselves and consequently the work is Stiff*'.

He was still very active in his missionary work and his diary entry for the 6th of May sees him at a prayer meeting at the west end of Locheport in a widow MacLellan's house where there was, '*A fair turnout*, [but I] *Had to do all the service myself singing & all.*'

Another meeting on May 17th in Carinish one evening sees him very pleased with the turnout of about sixty people. '*A blind man delivered a powerful and beautiful prayer. Though blind outwardly, he evidently has great "Light" inwardly ...*' He was assisted a few times by this man, a Mr MacLean, and is very impressed with his rhetoric, '[He] *is possessed of a very retentive memory and who seems to be walking in the great light of the Gospel though deprived of the use of the bodily eye.*'

There is an amusing episode in which he lost his door key on the way home one evening just as it got dark. He had obviously taken it from his pocket, about two hundred yards from the house, dropped it and despite a search, he was forced to put up at the house of a neighbour for the night. He searched in vain for it the next day, '*but to no purpose. Had to enter in the window for my Sabbath clothes.*' I think what is appealing and makes me smile is his understated restraint in his diary entry the day after; '*Found the key this morning and so I am up in spirits again*'. He was obviously very thankful to get home again, although mindful of the Good Samaritan who gave him shelter, '*Back to my own house tonight; I was welcomely received & kindly treated indeed at Archibald MacCuish's ...* '

During the next few days it became very cold and there were heavy snow showers. The snow continued to fall, May looked as if it had returned to winter and he remarked that warming his hands after reading and writing is somewhat unusual in May! On the 19th of May it was still pretty cold and he returned home from Clachan with a letter from his brother Alexander at home in Sutherland, which said,

> *they are removing from Achnaluachrach the dear old home to Davoch-Beg. Felt pretty sad all the evening at thought of never going back to spend any more happy days amongst the wild hills of Achnaluachrach. At times I sit considering whether it is not dreaming I am, and that there is no reality in it. But no, there it is before me in black and white 'on and after the 26th Inst. address all letters to Davoch-Beg, Rogart'.*

May remained cold and wet, but he still went off twice a week to Carinish to teach in his wee school there, where his pupils, well some of them, were making progress after only a fortnight of his being there.

> *Class I is making very satisfactory progress, especially the girls who are getting ahead of the boys. Class II is desperately stiff. What they learn one day is forgotten before I go back. They are still on the alphabet on small letters. Class III is composed of the youngest who are upon the alphabet on large (Capital) letters.*

He remarks on the whooping cough still lingering in the district.

Meanwhile, back at Locheport, the house he was living in was in a sad state of disrepair. So much so, it was now leaking badly and he woke one morning to find the rain splashing down on his head and pillow. In general, he was not terribly well looked after and although food was included in his stay, he was hungry quite a lot of the time as meal times after his breakfast could be erratic to say the least when he was out and about. In Carinish, if he was given a 'dinner' it was an event, as sometimes he could spend a whole day teaching there, with a prayer meeting afterwards, returning home ravenously hungry, having been offered nothing in the way of sustenance, '*At Claddach Carinish all day. Did not – as usual get anything to eat there. Returned raging with hunger or perhaps it was the hunger that was raging ...*'

It is also apparent that there was a great deal of apathy in the community and frankly George could not be doing with apathy. He set about getting his house re-thatched to keep the continuous, or so it seemed, rain from entering it. He organised a work force of young people to gather a large load of heather for this from a small island in the vicinity. There were two islands in the area well known for their good heather, Steiseidh and Rusgaidh (both names stemming from Old Norse).

The account of this expedition sounds hilarious. They all set off, fifteen of them, in a small very leaky boat. On arrival the whole party, with great glee, took off running all over the island in search of gulls eggs, although the season for them was well past, until recalled to their main purpose, whereupon they eventually set about cutting the heather for the roof thatching. Transporting it and themselves back across the loch was not without its difficulties either!

But even after this was gathered, the rain continued downwards and it was fully a week later and a rare dry day, when he persuaded them to at least thatch the part that was the worst … and still the rain fell. He was heartily sick of it. On one of his trips over to Carinish, it was so wet, that before he set off, he took his boots off and walked there barefoot so as to put them on and be dry and comfortable once he was there!

An invitation to a wedding three miles from Clachan brought a little light relief and with more curiosity than anything else, he accepted. After a long wait at the appointed house, the wedding party finally arrived and the festivities began with a large round of whisky, *'an element which seemed to get ample justice done to it throughout the night.'*

At 9.30pm they had their dinner, consisting of whisky, broth and fowl; then another round of whisky with a blessing and the men adjourned to the outdoors, the weather having become more clement. They were summoned inside again after about two hours to another dinner, this time of whisky, broth and mutton, the men being served first, the women afterwards.

The rest of the evening was passed in the singing of Gaelic songs, which considering the amount of whisky involved, would have been regaled, one imagines, with little restraint and much gusto by the company. He enjoyed the singing hugely and noted that all the company, taking each-others hands, beat time to the refrain upon their knees. Tea appeared at daybreak and as the sun came up everyone dispersed to their respective homes, himself included.

In early June he made a visit to Lochmaddy for the first time and although it was a small place, it had a bank, courthouse, hotel, poorhouse, shop and post office. To George, accustomed to living as he has for the past few months, it seemed like a small town. The *Dunara Castle* had just docked and he went down to join in the general buzz that a ship docking brings with it. He was even invited to have a meal with some new acquaintances he had been introduced to, which, he remarked, was <u>most</u> welcome before the long journey homewards.

Back home again, he went one evening for a sail in a local fisherman's boat where a strong breeze soon gets stronger still and he narrowly escaped being flung into the water

> *... a strong breeze blew which soon became a gale. Several times the boat was on its edge, and once about two barrels of water came in. As it was a small light boat the wonder is that we were not capsized into the sea. Being unacquainted with sailing I did not know I ran such a risk, but they were telling me afterwards.*

He ventured out with a local shepherd, named MacVicar, to climb to the top of Eaval, the highest hill in the area and was surprised when he got to the top at just how much water there was below, in the shape of numerous small lochans, sea lochs and inlets, and reflected with wonder on how everyone managed to get around in this terrain which was predominantly water. This is quite true as the whole of the Uists are over 60% water, people making do with what little land there is.

It was however, still raining and he was heartily tired of it, especially as he had to move to another bed and it was also damp. He was also cross, very cross, as the part which was worst for leaks was the part that was just newly thatched; a job obviously not well done. The next day was even worse and on June 11th he wrote,

> *... this morning has fairly outstrippt that of yesterday with respect to rain. Compelled to abandon the bed in which I took refuge yesterday. Rose and I sat at the fireside. House in a miserable state. Not a dry place. Rain running on the floor from closet to the fire – Clothes and books greatly damaged. I seldom saw such a day of rain ... only a few peats remained and these few were quite saturated with rain, so to add to inconveniences my fire was black and cold. With a slight alteration in Dante's line, I frequently repeated 'Abandon <u>comfort</u> all ye who enter here ...'*

The weather continued wet and showery with only the odd blink of sun, but eventually in mid-July a beautiful summer day dawned at last. It was a holiday in North Uist, with the annual Fair taking place in Lochmaddy, however taking advantage of the fine day, he eschewed the pleasure of a trip to town and spent most of it drying out his books and clothing in the warm sunshine. The fine weather continued and he remarked on just how depressing the past deluge has been on man and beast. The crops also were greatly damaged and many were now fully a month behind. This is quite serious as the further north, the shorter the growing season.

He managed to get to Paible on the west side of the island and remarked on how different it is there, '*The country in that part of the island presents quite a different aspect from the part we have the <u>misfortune</u> to be in. Paible and the surrounding townships are not mossy but sandy and green; good large crofts, comfortable houses, also farms.*' The minister there made him very welcome, was most hospitable and invited him to stay the night, but as George knew he had school to teach at Carinish the next day, he declined the invitation with much regret. He promised he would return to take up the offer later. We are left wondering if indeed he got there, as his North Uist diary concludes abruptly, '[July] *25th Very wet again, sorry I cannot return to Paible as I intended ...*'.

CLEITS AT MULLACH SGAR
WITH DUN – ST. KILDA – JUNE '08

One imagines his time from there on was taken up with a multitude of tasks; his school, Sunday school, prayer meetings etc. until the beginning of October, before boarding the steamer for home and the new house at Davochbeg. Perhaps he just ran out of steam, or the continuous rain was so depressing he was not disposed to write any more in his diary. It took him four days to eventually reach home.

Having set his path on course for the New College, Edinburgh and the ministry, he seems to have thrown himself into that life and all that it offered and it's not hard to imagine, on being put forward for the post of teacher for a year on the faraway island of St Kilda the following year, he accepted it with alacrity, the equivalent of today's 'gap year', before commencing his serious studying in Edinburgh's New College.

How marvellous it must have sounded to him. A whole year away on a remote island, a chance to help spread more of God's teachings to a small and (he presumed) receptive community, for there was a minister of his Church already out there, a Mr MacKay.

He probably thought, that in a modest way, he would be welcomed by Mr MacKay in helping bring a new and fresh approach to Church matters on the island and of course having had experience of taking and taking part in the services in North Uist, he very likely assumed that his role in St Kilda would include much of the same.

But as we read in the diary extracts, this turned out to be far from reality and George was obviously frustrated and bored with the monotonous fare dished out by the then aging Mr MacKay, who had no intention whatsoever of relinquishing any of his power and control of what he considered his island and flock. Neither could he reconcile himself to the obvious 'blinkered' and narrow views which Mr MacKay had of certain situations. George's innate sense of justice and fairness made him despair at times and in the latter part of his diary entries, it was obviously going to be a great relief to get away from St Kilda and its narrow confines; you can feel the anticipation and joy of homecoming, to what was for him, a sane world.

There is not much information about his immediate movements after St Kilda, but we next hear of him in The New College, Edinburgh as a student in training for the Free Church ministry. The 'Ladies' are still actively sending him on more field trips, but one gets the impression that islands have lost their glamour for George, as he pops up in a census in Applecross in Wester Ross as lodger and theology student and also in the Dingwall area. At last, in 1894, he was ordained and inducted into the Free Church of Scotland, Kilninver, in the parish of Kilninver and Kilmelford, twelve miles south of Oban, where he was to remain until 1902.

At the first disruption within the Church of Scotland in 1843, the 'breakaways' from that church, now the Free Church of Scotland, had built two churches in the area, one at Kilninver and the other at Kilmelford, which also had a school and school house.

Kilninver is a nice wee rural church of one and a half storeys. It is built on a small hill at the head of a sea loch and at the time of George's arrival it stood alone on the hill with a wide and open outlook, surrounded by heather and moorland hills, looking to the east across the loch and valley. The church is still there today; a holiday house, belonging to the Kilninver Estate and it is now surrounded by lush vegetation and trees.

The majority of the population in this area were Gaelic speaking and although the church ministers spoke English, they were expected to conduct services in Gaelic and indeed this trend was to continue right up until the 1950s. That may have appealed to him, as he was always seeking ways to improve his Gaelic. In his North Uist diary, in 1885, he was frustrated with himself for not being able to 'expound' in the language. This he more than makes up for in later years, as he becomes well known as a preacher of great Gaelic sermons.

Two years after his arrival in Kilninver, on the 11th of June at the Free Church in Dingwall, he married Catherine Macaskill or 'Katie' as she was affectionately known to the family. Katie was the daughter of the Rev. Murdoch Macaskill of Dingwall, a fiercely outspoken man, a great orator and completely unafraid of letting his opinions be known.

We are unsure how the two young people met, but there was at that time in the Highlands a large social structure within the Free Church. Part of this took the form and was known as the 'Communion Season'. Communion in the Free Church took place twice a year and in the Highlands it would begin with a 'fast day' on the Thursday before the Sabbath, followed by the Catechising of the congregation on the Friday and Saturday, then communion on the Sabbath. Mondays were reserved for Thanksgiving.

Many of the communions were taken by travelling ministers and obviously the best time for them to fulfil these duties would be in the summer months, when travel was a lot easier than in wintertime. Congregations treated these as a form of holiday and whole congregations would uproot and travel on foot quite large distances, sometimes as much as fifty miles, to attend these in other parishes, some attending three or four or more, travelling from parish to parish. It was a great way to socialise with old friends and meet new people and many marriages were the result. Who knows how George and Katie met, but we do hear of him in the Dingwall area, possibly on a field trip, the year before his ordination.

At any rate George, now aged thirty-six, settled down to life in the Kilninver and Kilmelford parish and it was there that three of their children were born. In a 1901 census of Kilninver and Kilmelford, Argyll, their address is given as: The UFC Manse, Melford Road. George is forty-one, Katie thirty, their first child Jessie Victoria, (known as 'Ria') is three and son John, (known as 'Iain') is one, with Agnes a very new baby. There is also a servant, Sarah Campbell, aged fifteen.

Regarding this census, it is very interesting to note that the address is the United Free Church Manse and not the Free Church Manse. George it appears is now a minister of the UFC.

To go back to two years before George's arrival at Kilninver, there had already been a few rumblings within the Free Church and much difference of opinion from various ministers. There had been published in 1891 a Declaratory Act, setting out their constitution, which appeared to some in the ministry to contain considerable vagueness and ambiguity and its wording was painstakingly picked apart by some members who liked to have clear and concise boundaries relating to any changes within the Free Church doctrines. The ensuing political and doctrinal manoeuvrings caused two church ministers to secede from the Free Church to form the Free

Presbyterian Church. Several students joined them and as the ministers were from Raasay and Shieldaig, a considerable number of congregations in the Highlands also joined them. George would have known about this only too well.

By 1895, a divisive spirit had entered the Free Church and at that year's General Assembly, the main body within the Free Church decided to form a Union committee to effect negotiations to integrate the minority dissenters back into the fold, but also paving the way for some constitutional changes.

George's father-in-law, the Rev. Macaskill, was a very outspoken critic of the Declamatory Act and at a General Assembly in 1897 he had declared his views on the subject, but Dr Rainy, heading the General Assembly and an adroit speaker, perpetrator and upholder of the Act, persuaded him to accept it and he found himself being appointed as a member of the Union committee and its subsequent overtures to the dissenters.

In 1898, the dissenters objected vociferously to the changes proposed by the committee. Their main objections were that the changes were at variance to the basic doctrines of the Free Church set up in 1843 and they argued further, that not only was the Act unlawful in that it could not change a constitution once set up, but that this Act in its vagueness and ambiguity opened the doors to overtures from the Church of Scotland, waiting, with extreme interest in the wings.

Later in that same year (1898), the General Assembly of the Free Church held a two day conference in Inverness on 'The Deepening of Spiritual Life', but in reality it was held to try to offset the damage done by the small group of dissenters within its own doors. George would definitely have attended this, for it was not often the General Assembly was held there and it would have been a great opportunity to hear first-hand great speakers of the day in doctrinal matters. George was always a scholar, with a scholar's mindset.

In the 1900 Disruption there was an official declaration from the Free Church that the new United Free Church, which was now being brought into being, was simply an enlargement of the Free Church established in 1843. The now minority dissenters, twenty seven ministers in total, much less than a third of the existing Free Church, were appalled. They insisted that theirs was the true church and the new United Free was unlawful as the original constitution could not be changed. Furthermore, they declared that this was the slippery slope towards the Church of Scotland. They were standing firm as the one true Free Church. The stark reality of the situation was, that far from promoting a union beneficial to all, the Free Church majority had in effect, by forcing this union upon its members, caused such dissent, as to successfully divide it into three parts; the Free Presbyterian Church of 1893, the United Free Church of 1900 and the continuing Free Church of Scotland of 1843.

The disruption it caused was particularly violent and acrimonious. Battle, literally, commenced and overnight ministers who had entered into the United Free Church union claimed possession of most of all the Free Church manses and churches. The Free Church members were horrified. Not only had their faith, they felt, been tampered with, but their property seemed to have been confiscated as well and they were now homeless. It was a period of extreme harassment on the part of the UFC. Stipends were cut off, pensions and monetary obligations axed without explanation or sympathy and without thought of the hardships that would ensue. Several Church of Scotland ministers charitably offered their buildings to homeless congregations and amongst some of the UFC ministers, there were quite a few who disassociated themselves from this unkind and arrogant treatment meted out by the majority of the UFC to the 'Wee Frees' as the Free Church minority were known. One assumes that George was one of those, as he was an extremely kind person with a very highly developed moral sense of justice and fairness.

The upheaval abating slightly, George and his family decided to move to the Parish of Tarbat in Portmahomack in Easter Ross in 1902. It was nearer both their homes; George's father was failing, and Katie no doubt was glad also to be nearer her family, but perhaps during these stirring times George just wanted to be a bit closer to the action that was taking place and had felt a bit isolated in Kilninver.

Their own family was growing and they left on the 28th of October to go to a fine manse and church in Portmahomack and settled down. Their peace did not last long. George was a popular man and he had the knack of making friends wherever he went, but he never lost his abhorrence of conflict and violence. It is not that he was incapable of dealing with it; he just would have preferred that there was none. Around his church and parish at this time windows were being broken, hayricks burned to the ground, property destroyed in the name of the church and it says much of his greatness of spirit, that, it was recorded at the height of the hostilities, he preached a very moving and heartfelt sermon on tolerance, forgiveness and understanding. A very brave thing to do in these troubled times.

The original Free Church members meantime had decided to challenge the UFC on legal matters, including the return of their property. Dr Rainy promptly offered them £50,000 in compensation, a huge sum of money in those days. They spurned it, considering it a bribe. They then took their claims to the Court of Session where they were rejected. They appealed and their claims were again rejected. Undaunted, for they were convinced they were right, they managed to scrape up the necessary funds, no mean feat, and took their appeal to the highest court in the land; the House of Lords.

After many months of debate, their cause was finally upheld and the decision was published on the 1st of August 1904 in their favour. The name, 'Free Church of Scotland' it was declared, 'belonged to the minority who, holding to the church's Constitution and Standards, had declined to be a party to a compromising Union.' With the greatest glee and delight they set about reversing their situation. Almost overnight George and his family were evicted from their church and manse out into the street. George had another daughter by this time, Jane, less than a year old. It seemed a double blow to them as George's father had died at Davochbeg earlier that year in June, aged seventy-four.

The congregation however, rallied round; a flat above a shop on the shores of Portmahomack was given to the family to live in and a subscription set up for the building of a new church and manse; the church being finally completed in 1908. They were well taken care of, for George was much

CLEITS -
VILLAGE BAY
ST. KILDA FEB '08

loved and respected, but it was while they were in their temporary home in 1906 that Katie suffered a 'turn'. We don't know what form this 'turn' took, but we know that she eventually went on to contract Multiple Sclerosis (MS), so it is likely that this was an early symptom of the disease, perhaps a numbness of her arms and hands affecting her grip, or more likely her balance had been affected. She had two more children, Katharine in 1907 and George in 1909.

The family moved again in 1912. This time to the parish of Petty near Nairn. There they finally settled down away from the conflicts and life seems to have been a bit easier for them. Katie unfortunately was succumbing inexorably to her MS, but the children throve.

Then came the Great War of 1914, which sent the whole country into a state of upheaval. George's eldest son John (Iain) enlisted in the Black Watch when he finished his schooling in 1917 and went off to fight on the front line in France. George himself was not slow in taking up war duties as a church minister and we believe he may have served for a spell as chaplain to some of the troops stationed in nearby Inverness, although in his obituary in the Northern Times, it says 'he did duty for some months as a chaplain at the front', we are pretty certain he wasn't in France.

In the spring of 1918, always thinking of others and how best to serve them, he is composing a new form of worship service for soldiers returning home. Then, on the 8th of July, the Rev. George Murray died suddenly after suffering an accident involving a window, which appears to have fallen on him.

Even the family are a bit hazy as to what actually happened. Some reports indicate that it was a sash window that had come down on him; others said it was a rotten window frame in an outbuilding or a skylight falling down suddenly. The obituary in the Northern Times simply says, 'while standing in his room in the manse, he was struck by a falling window which afflicted an injury to the head.' Whatever happened to him, it was thought that at first he was just suffering from concussion, but two days later he died having suffered a major haemorrhage to the brain.

He was interred in the churchyard of Petty, attended by a large congregation, with many eminent churchmen assisting in the service. Amongst the chief mourners were of course his family from Rogart. His eldest son was still in France fighting for his country and Katie was at this time an invalid, her mobility severely impaired, having the comfort of her daughters and her son George, who was just eight years old to see her through this awful time. The obituaries in both the Northern Times and the Inverness Courier are lavish in their praise of the Rev. George.

The Courier quotes the Rev. MacGillivray, who said of him,

> Mr Murray's personality was charming and sympathetic. He was always good natured, warm hearted and affectionate, in him there dwelt no unclean thought, no selfish ambition, no littleness, no meanness. Possessed of a large charity, he judged no man harshly, but on the contrary strove to bring out the best points, to eliminate the disagreeable qualities and excuse the worst defects of those from whom he differed. One parted

> from him with a keener zest for life and with a stronger faith in
> the goodness of human nature. His was in every sense, a useful
> life – a life full of many interests and activities.
>
> A faithful preacher, he broke the bread of life to his hearers
> seriously and diligently. A regular visitor, he was as sincerely
> welcomed in the homes of the parish church congregation as he
> was among his own people. His only desire was to serve, his joy
> to help those on whom the burden of life pressed too heavily,
> and he was ever ready to give his aid where it was needed.

A beautiful and fitting tribute to him.

The family moved to Inverness to a house given by the church. A sister of Katie's came to look after the family and the children began school there. Katie finally succumbed to her MS aged 59 and passed from this life on the 5th of July 1931 at 38 Lovat Road, Inverness.

George lives on in his diary of St Kilda, parts of which have appeared in so many publications, including this one. He is still the subject of debate and interest and perhaps this brief history of his life and the North Uist diary content will reveal much more of this earnest and much loved man, for in the old and much worn aphorism 'the likes of him will never be again.'

How true.

Part Two

The St Kilda Diary 1886-87

BORERAY AND THE STACS
ST KILDA – JUNE '08

S T KILDA made a huge impression on George; it certainly shocked him. The rawness of the landscape, the primitive, almost savageness of its people and their harsh struggle for survival on that barren rock contributed to that impression. St Kilda already had a church and minister of his own denomination; a Mr MacKay, who although elderly and, it was rumoured, not in the best of health, nevertheless had been there for twenty years. A fresh approach from an enthusiastic young man on his way to becoming a minister himself would probably be appreciated by both minister and congregation and although his principal role would be as a teacher, he was not averse to assisting in spiritual matters. With his North Uist experience behind him, he assumed modestly that he would be welcomed.

Meanwhile, as he waited patiently for the call to set off for the island, he was happily embarked upon chores at the new family farm at Davochbeg. His steamer trunk would have been packed and ready with everything to sustain him for a whole year in the wilds and he was also taking a quantity of books for study. His Gaelic had improved enormously and he was much more confident in his abilities of articulation in this sphere.

The actual diary begins very simply. It is written in the same ruled exercise book as the North Uist entries the year before and I am indebted to Jennifer Murray Reid, George's granddaughter, for the meticulous care she has taken in correcting Mr James Fisher's original transcript of 1947, working closely from George's original diary to ensure that this transcript is absolutely accurate and exactly as he wrote it.

1886 ST. KILDA Teacher.

July 27th. On April 2nd I left Aberdeen for Rogart after my third session in Arts. Passed all the Exams. & took my M.A. in Classics.

I engaged during the spring with the "Ladies Association" to go out to St. Kilda as teacher for the next twelve months. At home I had to remain till the sailing of a vessel from Dunvegan, Skye. Two months I spent at home very happily, acting as shepherd and gardener.

It was on 5th June at 3 P.M. that I received a telegram to start at once for Dunvegan as the vessel sailed on Monday.

On Saturday morning the 6th at 7 a.m., I left Rogart for St. Kilda. I felt not a little sad leaving home on that occasion as I did not expect being back for a twelvemonth at least, nor did I know what might befall me on such a long and perilous journey.

On arriving at Stromeferry, I had to take the mail gig all the way to Portree as the steamer did not sail on Saturday.

Starting from Stromeferry at 4 p.m. we passed over mountains, alongside lochs and down valleys till we reached Kyle of Kin [Lochalsh] *where we had to cross a ferry about a ¼ mile broad. On the other side the mail gig was waiting, and off we set for Broadford, where we rested for nearly an hour. I had a cup of tea in the Inn. Resuming our journey we passed through beautiful scenery in "the isle of the Mist" (Skye).*

12 o'clock Saturday night found us travelling right at the foot of the Cuchullins [Cuillins]. *The night was calm & not a sound was to be heard save the rattling of the gig wheels as it slowly ascended the hills. The scene at midnight in summer was grand. On the left the Cuchullins rose up so majestically & had gone to sleep for the night with a "Scotch Mist" for a nightcap. On the right was the still clear water* [Loch Sligachan].

Not till 2.30 a.m. Sabbath morning did we reach Portree. Tired and fatigued I was no doubt. Got into the "Portree Hotel" but had to walk off to bed cold and hungry as I was.

On Monday morning at 5 o'clock I resumed my journey, without getting a bite of breakfast, en route for Dunvegan, where I arrived at 9 a.m., a distance of 25 miles. I omitted to say that the distance bet. Stromeferry & Portree is about fifty miles. Thus I made 75 miles by mail gig, for which I paid only 18/6 or 3d. per mile for myself & my trunk. Had to put in Dunvegan Hotel for 2 days, as the vessel was not ready for sailing. Went on board the "Robert Hadden" on Tuesday night. Not a breath of wind & so we did not move till early next morning. On the whole we had a fine passage, rather calm the first day. After passing through the Sound of Harris on Wednesday night we got into the open Atlantic & a strong favourable breeze blew. Though the vessel was small & the sea running pretty high I did not feel sick in the least.

On rising out of my hammock on Thursday morning at 7 I had presented before me the island of St. Kilda & already we were entering the bay. Calm as the weather now was, the landing was no small difficulty.

It would be at Dunvegan that George would have met his fellow passengers who were to sail with him to the island; MacLeod of Macleod's Factor, a Mr MacKenzie and his son, on their way out to collect the annual rents and Robert Connell from the Glasgow Herald. Robert Connell was a journalist, or as he liked to style himself, 'Special Correspondent'. He had been to St Kilda once before and had forceful and decided opinions of the people and the island. His previous visit had been in response by his newspaper and private subscriptions, to letters of distress from a scholar and the minister Mr MacKay in September the year before.

These had been received via St Kilda mailboats and had been washed up on beaches in the Western Isles and the contents forwarded to the various addressees.

St Kilda mailboats were of recent invention and were sent out in times of distress. They were small wooden boxes with a sealed bottle or tin containing a letter or letters. The boxes would have the words 'St Kilda Mail Please Open' burnt onto them, a float would be attached and they would be consigned to the sea and tides with the hope of arriving on the opposite shore and being picked up.

Robert Connell had been chosen to accompany the 'relief supplies' sent out in the October, with a view to reporting on the true nature of the islanders' distress, which would satisfy his employers, the Glasgow Herald, and the private subscribers who had hired and paid for the *Hebridean* steam ship and food for the destitute islanders. The supplies having been landed, he had gone on to interview various personages and had returned to Glasgow to publish his report.

By all accounts the report was unclear as to their actual distress and dwelt mostly on their peculiarities and customs. He did report that the islanders had begged him most earnestly to send them more supplies, as they said what he had brought would scarcely see them through the winter. Meanwhile he was now once more on his way back out to ascertain the state of the community and how they had fared. His own views, which he would have made known to his sailing companions, were that the best solution for those strange, primitive and uncivilised natives was for them to be sent to the colonies, thus leaving the island free for other enterprises such as a Fisheries factory or other industrial undertakings, as St Kilda inhabitants were a great burden to the British tax payer.

George would have been shocked and disgusted by Connell's complete lack of good manners and total disregard for the feelings of the poor islanders. (George also discovered later, that when on the island, Connell had made himself objectionable by prying intrusively into their family lives, wishing to conduct interviews on the Sabbath and other totally inappropriate times.)

In other words we get the impression that Connell was filled to the brim with his own smug self-importance and superior moralistic views on what should be done with St Kilda and its inhabitants. It's not at all difficult to imagine the two MacKenzies being in accord with George in their dislike of Connell. It must have been an awkward journey for all four!

On shore at last, the arrival of the Factor seems to have been ill timed as a party of islanders had gone over to Boreray to 'pluck' the fleeces of the sheep out there. As well as a church Elder, they had also taken with them a woman to assist secure the fleeces and cook for them. They had only been gone a few days and were not expected to return for at least a week, the changeability of the weather being the only threat to their return. The Factor would have to wait for them before concluding his business and as most years this took around ten days to carry out, it didn't seem to be that much of a misfortune.

Robert Connell, it appears, immediately urged that a boat be put out to bring them back forthwith; this the people refused to do, saying that once the signal was received to say they were ready, they would be brought off and not before.

George meanwhile would have met with Hugh MacCallum, the teacher he was to replace and who would have been very anxious to get home. George was to lodge in the Factor's house and what with Hugh, himself and the two MacKenzies and all their gear, plus the housekeeper, it must have been a trifle cramped. He would have been officially welcomed by the minister Mr MacKay, whose sister also resided in the manse. By all accounts she was a poor soul, elderly and very feeble, taking not much interest in her surroundings. His diary carries on:

> *On Sabbath night, the 25th July, at 11 o'clock Finlay Gillies, the oldest man on the island, died of palsy, by which he was suddenly attacked the Wednesday previous. He had reached the advanced age of eighty years, was an inoffensive quiet man and had the use of all his faculties till Wednesday. His sufferings were great up till the time he died. This twenty seventh day of July 1886 Finlay Gillies,*

aged 80 years, was interred in the south side of the cemetery, in the grave where his first wife was buried fifty two years ago. From the appearance of the bones, this woman must have been of great size and strength. Nor was she but young when she departed this life. The teeth were still quite white & I failed to remove them from the jaw. A solemn ceremony it was & in some respects peculiar to the place. The women followed the remains to the grave, where they sat weeping & moaning till the earth, heaped on, hid from them the body of him whose departure they lamented. On looking through the churchyard, I felt sad at the sight of so many infant graves. One man, not yet fifty years, I should say, pointed the place to me where he buried nine children. He is left with four of a family. Another buried no less than a dozen infants and is left with two, now grown up. Sad to think of the like. Bad treatment at birth must have been the cause of so many dying.

We now know this to have been tetanus, which was endemic in the soil and habitations on the island. He was partly right, in that they were not all that hygienic in many of their tasks and this was compounded with the fact that there were rumours of strange rituals at the time of birth; for example, it is said that the umbilical cord was anointed with the oil of the fulmar kept in the preserved stomach of the bird, which cannot have done much to get the infants off to a good start in life. The islanders themselves seem to have had a fatalistic view of it all and it was accepted as part of everyday life, or in this case; death. They were so steeped in their own traditions and customs as to repel any changes suggested and it was not until a good ten to fifteen years later that nurses sent to the island began, forcibly, to make inroads and introduce better health and hygiene to eradicate this problem.

28th Calm sultry day with south breeze in evening.

29th Pouring rain all day. The wettest day I saw yet in St. Kilda.

30th Warm calm day. Fishing round Dun in evening.

31st Morning rather dark. Cleared up by nine o'clock. Went to Soa [Soay] with the men to snare puffins. The day was not favourable for snaring. I got ten. Not so bad for the first trial. Seeing that we were making nothing at the snaring we set off to catch sheep. We had no dogs so we had to run over the rocks and drive them into crevices, where they were caught, hard & dangerous work. I saw two caught on a precipice by throwing a rope over their necks and pulling them off. The Soa sheep are of a peculiar colour, generally brown on the back & white below. They are very wild and appeared like a lot of roes or young deers on the rocks. Arrived home at 7.30 PM, pretty hungry.

Augt 4th. Up till this evening we had good weather, though showers occasionally. Last night we had the monthly prayer meeting and tonight the weekly one. At the close the Revd. Mr. McKay drew the attention of the people to the Irish question. He is much surprised at Mr Gladstone going so far wrong in his old age.

The Irish question had its roots in the twelfth century, when the British imposed a feudal landowning system on Ireland. Noblemen, many of them absentee, were granted estates and large tracts of land, which they in turn rented out to farm workers and labourers in exchange for crops and services. The landowners levied high rents on their tenants, most of who descended into abject poverty and social deprivation. The landlords however, became extremely wealthy on the backs of these poor people. Social problems became worse around the 1700s when the English tried to impose the Protestant faith on Ireland in opposition to the Roman Catholics, who were in the majority.

In 1801 the Act of Union united England and Ireland, forming the United Kingdom. Scottish and English Protestant settlers were encouraged to populate this new Ireland and as a result Ulster, which is where the majority settled, became mostly Protestant with a decidedly Protestant character.

Ulster and the north, with more new English and Scottish wealth to invest, became industrialised and progressive, while the South remained Catholic and agricultural.

During the 1840s the Potato Famine struck Ireland, resulting in over a million deaths. Many Irish blamed this catastrophe on the Corn Laws introduced by the British Government; forcing the Irish farmers to export their corn to Britain, with the result that most turned to growing potatoes with its ensuing disastrous consequences. In 1858 the Fenian Movement was formed to try to achieve Irish Independence, but Britain managed to repress, for the time being, anything of a rebellious nature.

For the remainder of the 19th century, politicians, such as the British Prime Minister, William Gladstone (1809–1898) and the Irish Nationalist leader, Charles Parnell (1846–1891), made several unsuccessful attempts to gain self-government for Ireland. Gladstone genuinely desired to improve the lot of the Irish peasantry and he became increasingly focussed on this. He began to advocate 'Home Rule' for Ireland which was, in most people's opinion, exceedingly radical and not at all popular. During Gladstone's time in government, in order to diffuse an increasingly tense political situation, he managed to disestablish the Church of Ireland (Protestant), which meant that Catholics no longer had to pay tithes to the Anglican Church in England; in other words he was seen to be encouraging and supporting the Catholics. No wonder then, that Mr MacKay was moved to comment on this. George's opinion, possibly, would have been much the same as MacKay's but I think he would also have seen the wider picture, in that Gladstone sought peace and an end to conflict.

> *5th Terrible stormy morning. Had just rung the bell when the "Hebridean" hove in sight and off we went to put out the boat.*
>
> *So stormy was the shore that we hesitated for a moment to consider whether or not it was safe to venture. Against the will of many men & women about ten of us set off & reached the vessel in safety. This was at 9.30am.*
>
> *Not till between 3 & 4 o'clock did we return, nor did the passengers venture to land till then. On board there were many passengers, amongst whom was Miss Rainy, who shortly after landing examined the school and was well pleased with the way in which the scholars acquitted themselves in the respective subjects.*

As well as the usual tourists on board the ship, the owner of St Kilda, MacLeod of MacLeod, arrived with a small entourage on that stormy day. He had come for a prolonged stay of a few weeks to see how the island and his people were faring. He was put up in the manse and the rest of his people were found lodgings elsewhere, several ending up in the Factor's house with George.

6th Held school. Fine in the forenoon. Showers later on in the day. Distributed sweets.

7th (Saturday). Forenoon spent outside with Mr. McLeod, who photographed the men mending a boat & me reading a letter to them. In the afternoon I wrote letters for the people and read papers.

8th Fair & calm. Had the privilege of hearing an English sermon.

9th Fine calm day.

Augt 10th Morning calm & clear. From 12.15 – 1.30 pouring rain. Men & Mr. McLeod [sic] in Boreray. They had no rain. After school I called upon the Revd. Mr. McKay, relative to Mr. McNeil's report on St. Kilda. The recalling to memory of these reports caused such a disturbance in the Manse that I wished at one time I could vanish into thin air. Ignorant people ruling in a manse! Prior to our taking up McNeil's report, I heard what I hold as gross superstition, the greatest rubbish of tales.

MacLeod, in the course of conversations with George, would in all probability have touched on the subject of the McNeill report. George may well have previously heard of this, as there was a great deal of correspondence relating to the subject in all the press at the time of its publication in March. He may have heard a little from Hugh MacCallum, but it appears nothing had been mentioned by Mr MacKay. MacLeod would have wanted to put George in possession, as he saw it, of a full account of the affair and the truth of what had actually happened.

The story was thus: the previous year, MacLeod's Factor had arranged with the *Robert Hadden*, at the end of the summer, that the usual winter supplies of meal, tea, sugar and other commodities would be delivered to the island. This was the normal way things were done and there were enough supplies ordered to last them till the following April. These had been dispatched, and had arrived safely on the island. Then in September a Mr Kenneth Campbell, the schoolteacher prior to Hugh MacCallum, residing now in Lewis, had received a letter. It had been found in a bottle, which in turn had been enclosed in a little wooden boat, which had been washed up on the shore. It was from one of the pupils of Hugh, saying that a great storm had swept over the island and all the crops had been destroyed. A boat had been broken to pieces, he had written, and 'we are all near dead with hunger'.

This had caused quite a stir, but it was concluded that it had been a schoolboy's prank. Nothing more was thought of the matter until a week later, when two more letters, sent by the same method, turned up on the

AN LAG - ST. KILDA .

shores of the Outer Hebrides, this time written by the Reverend MacKay and dated 16th of September. One was addressed to a Free Church minister in Lochalsh, while the other was to Dr Rainy, Principal of the Free Church College in Edinburgh. Both were of similar content and corroborated the schoolboy's letter, that the island had suffered a vicious storm. It had taken away all the islanders' crops and destroyed a boat. Mr MacKay had examined all sixteen households and they appeared to be in desperate straits. He asked for immediate relief.

MacLeod had been in Paris at the time and had, on hearing the news, despatched word to the effect that his Factor was more than capable of dealing with the situation in his absence. Dr Rainy however, had treated the letter from Mr MacKay with great seriousness and had at once written to the government to ask for assistance for the poor unfortunate islanders. The HMS *Jackal* had responded to government authority and had set sail with the necessary supplies on board. The government had also sent, besides a Commander of the Royal Navy, another gentleman, Mr Malcolm McNeill, a former secretary to the Crofters Commission, now an Inspecting Officer of the Board of Supervision. He was commissioned to report on the true state and conditions he found out there and with his experience, the government was sure he would be able to produce an accurate report.

Meanwhile, before the *Jackal* could set sail; The *Hebridean* had been commissioned privately to set sail at once to St Kilda with relief supplies of oatmeal, oats and potatoes, tea, sugar etc. This vessel left before the *Jackal*, with Robert Connell, a special reporter from the Glasgow Herald on board. The supplies were landed safely.

The *Jackal* dropped anchor in Village Bay the day after Robert Connell's report appeared in the Glasgow Herald newspaper. Mr McNeill and Commander Osborne once ashore, immediately had a meeting with the Reverend MacKay and relevant parties and then Mr McNeill spoke to the islanders themselves. He returned to the mainland to write up his findings for the government.

The report was published in March and in it he concluded that not all the crops had been lost. Their potatoes had survived and the boat in question had been old and unseaworthy. There were still four good boats left and in good repair. They seemed to have ample supplies as their normal winter supplies had already been delivered and as well as the supplies from the *Hebridean* and the *Jackal*; they had more than a sufficiency of food and other commodities.

McNeill had also noted that a good few hundred visitors and tourists had visited the island that year and the St Kildians had earned a substantial amount of money from the sale of merchandise and wares produced by themselves. He had been very thorough and had decided that the islanders were luxuriously provided for and well able to face the winter ahead with fortitude.

MacLeod felt that Mr MacKay had been hoodwinked by the islanders and their greed. He would likely have referred to the influence of a certain Ewan Gillies, an emigrant returnee to St Kilda, who, in his opinion, had caused nothing but trouble since his return and had incited and infected the islanders with discontent. MacLeod would have felt that he had been more than generous to his tenants, but he was not to be taken in by their 'games', as had the Reverend MacKay.

George would have been deeply shocked and probably could not believe that the islanders had been so deceitful; hence his hurried visit to the manse for reassurance, which was not forthcoming; in fact he appears to have been horrified over the ensuing row.

Mr MacKay's housekeeper, Ann MacDonald, was extremely vociferous on every subject and would not have held back her views; indeed it was said of her that, '... she had a tongue which galloped and rattled like the paddles of a steamer ...', she also appears to have been firmly in control over everyone in the manse, she was well known to be a domineering woman and unfortunately seems to have been concerned in most of the rows and upsets that ensued throughout George's sojourn.

Regarding 'the greatest rubbish of tales', the islanders were extremely superstitious and the least thing; for example, some strange migratory birds appearing, any strange noises outside in the night, unusual behaviour amongst themselves, was noted and immediately attributed to supernatural forces. George certainly thought this was nonsense and did

not believe in the supernatural in any shape or form. These tales were no
doubt from the housekeeper.

*11ᵗʰ At 11.15am I suddenly dismissed the school & set out with the men
& Mr. McLeod* [sic] *for Boreray. A terrible sight to see the men go over
the rocks in quest of birds! A strange life indeed and one fraught with
great danger. I would not be satisfied till I should try the rope myself, so
on I got & over. Hanging between the sky and earth on a strong rope I
set to and performed the part of a fowler. Over cliffs & along ledges I &
other two went till, I am sure, we went down about 1,000 feet. The birds
were plentiful & we did well. I shouldered twenty fulmars & two solan
geese and began the ascent, which was no easy matter. A terrible shower
of rain fell as we were getting into the boat, in which Mr. McLeod and
Norman Gillies sat fishing all day and caught one mullet. Got home at
9.30pm pretty tired.*

12ᵗʰ Fine clear day. Men fowling on Mainland. [He means the main
island of Hirta] *I fished on the rocks in evening & got nothing.*

*13ᵗʰ. Fair though blowing a breeze. In evening went to Conacher to see
the men fowling. Evening dull & looked like rain.*

*14ᵗʰ Another notable day in my life. At 10am. six, including Mr. McLeod
and myself, set off with a boat round the island to pick up the birds the
men were pitching over the rocks above. There was a heavy swell and
consequently it was with danger to our lives that we approached the rocks.
I thought several times that the boat would be swamped. Worked with my
jacket off and sleeves up all day. Saw a young fulmar fly off.*

*15ᵗʰ. (Sabbath) Heard two short English sermons. Mr. McLeod in church
in forenoon & afternoon. Very stormy morning, great deal of rain. In the
evening it became calm though misty.*

' 'D fhuair sibh cadal math? [We're not sure what this reference
alludes to, as roughly translated it means 'Did you get a good sleep']

16th. Morning fair. Evening wet & misty. Went in afternoon to the Camber and killed a good few fulmars. Had the rope on me on the cliffs.

17th. Very fine day, hot in fact. Most of the men on the Dun. Went in evening to back of Conacher where four men were busy. Went down the steep & brought up burdens. It was no easy matter. It was perhaps the most hazardous place I went to yet. I was hanging for a moment or two in the air on two ropes over a cliff. Not a very nice sensation, I may say, notwithstanding that I had full confidence in the three girls & lad that were above holding the ropes. A number of young fulmars have been seen to fly today.

18th. Thick mist all day. In evening wrote letters.

20th. Fine calm day. Helped the men at towing in a whale from the Dun. We got it dead and had a hard pull. Tail 8 feet broad. Length of whale 28 feet

There were always whales in the area when I was on St Kilda. Sometimes the helicopter pilot would make a small detour on the way in or out to the island for us to see a pod of Minke whales, porpoise and other cetaceans. Minke were the most common we saw. Once we came across a very large dead decomposing whale, much larger than the Minke. We cruised round above it a few times, but no one was sure which species it was.

One never to be forgotten time, out on the slopes of Oiseval with the warden, I saw the elusive Blue whale cruise by, far out from the entrance to Village Bay. There were sometimes, but not very often, Orcas around, terrifying to watch in action. I once observed a small pod playing with a seal they'd caught off Ruaival. It was flung from one to the other in the manner of a rag doll. On Cape Wrath, years ago in winter, I saw from the lighthouse tower a huge pod of around thirty or forty, travelling noisily at great speed round the headland and on up the Pentland Firth where they were lost to sight.

We were sitting in the dining room on St Kilda one Saturday afternoon, lazily finishing lunch on a lovely summer's day, when the archaeologist came in to tell us there was a large pod of dolphin hunting in the bay. There were around fifteen cruising round in a large circle. The loud splashing noise they were making was extraordinary. From the occasional glimpse of rising fish in the middle of this circle it appeared they had driven a shoal of fish into the shelter of the bay and were now circling their prey. As we watched, the circle got smaller and smaller, the fish more frantic, then the dolphins dived as one and that was that! We didn't even see them head back out to sea; they had just ... gone, but what a memorable sight.

The whale that George helped tow back to the beach could have been one of any number of species. Having looked at the whale population that were prevalent in the area in the late 1800s, there were many in and around these waters. It would have been a great find as the blubber, once rendered down, would have been valuable as fuel for their lamps; it appears the islanders certainly knew what to do with it.

Augt 21ˢᵗ Fine warm day. "Dunara" arrived in the afternoon, having on board a great number of passengers, amongst whom were two doctors, who set a sprained foot, giving me instructions how it was to be managed afterwards. Besides one of them left a box of medicines. Got a box from home and a letter inside saying that they are all well and very busy.

22ⁿᵈ Bright warm day.

23ʳᵈ Forenoon fair with strong breeze. Evening misty with showers.

24ᵗʰ Wet in the afternoon.

25ᵗʰ Very wet the most of the day. Men busy taking the blubber off the whale.

26ᵗʰ Warm. Bright sunshine. Shower of rain at 10pm. Men at Soa for fulmar. An occasional puffin still to be seen. Fulmars leaving the island.

27ᵗʰ Calm bright day. Heavy rain at 9pm. Held school for 1 1/2 hours and then set out with the men for Soa. On reaching, we could not get landed. Two managed with difficulty to do so; but really I thought we would be drowned amongst the terrible waves that roared & dashed against the rocks.

Augt 28ᵗʰ Very stormy morning with rain and a strong gale. Terrible breakers out at sea. Towards midday it calmed considerably. Wrote letters to Australia for four parties.

There had been an emigration to Australia in 1852 of some thirty-six islanders and letters from relatives there arrived from time to time.

29ᵗʰ Fine sunny day. Mist & slight shower in evening.

30ᵗʰ The torrents of rain that fell today were extraordinary. I seldom, or never, saw a day like it at this time of the year. Very heavy sea on.

31ˢᵗ Still wet.

Septr 1ˢᵗ (Wednesday) Sometime about 1.30 or 2am., one of the heaviest showers of rain that ever I saw or heard passed over the island. It came down you would think in bucket fulls and in five minutes there was a stream passing the front of the house. Occasional showers through the day.

I'm not sure why, but the rain on Hirta when very heavy, did indeed present an extraordinary sight. It looked as if a continuous sheet of water was descending from the skies and being blown in to the hills. The small burns very soon became torrents and water ran down off the slopes in a multitude of streams. It was usually of short duration and once the shower ceased and the water had run down into the sea, the whole island looked as if it had never arrived in the first place.

2ⁿᵈ Beautiful day, calm & sunny. Not for a long time had we such a fine day. At 12.30 the "Hebridean" arrived with a number of passengers. As she did not leave till midnight the visitors had a proper day of it.

They bought a deal of cloth & stockings from the natives. Before they parted with us they & all the inhabitants of St. Kilda assembled outside the minister's garden just as [it] was getting dark. The whole together constituted a small congregation. Three Gaelic tunes were sung at the request of one of the strangers. Then, in English, we sang the Hundredth Psalm & the Hymn "How my comrades see the signal", after which the minister prayed in Gaelic. It was an evening I will long remember, with not so much as a breath of wind to drive the sound one way more than another, there we stood under the cloudless canopy of heaven singing "<u>All</u> people that on Earth &c". Few as we are on this remote island, it is comforting to think that we can, in unison with the rest of the world, "Sing to the Lord with cheerful voice".

With the steamer arrived from Australia an old man and a comparatively young wife. They intend remaining now in their native land.

3rd Had no school as I had no less than 23 letters to read for myself besides some through the village. All my relatives & acquaintances are well, which cheers my heart. Beautiful day again.

Septr 4th A third sunny day, calm & fair with a beautiful sky. These past three days did immense good to the crops. Bad as the weather was we see the Lord's promise, that as long as the world lasts there will be seed time & <u>harvest</u> is not to fail. "His promises are Yea and Amen". Went with the men to Boreray to catch sheep. The day was warm and I pitied the poor men running all day after the brutes that were almost as wild as deer. I helped to the best of my ability. Returned at 7.30 got washed, refreshed with meat, & then went to see Kate's sprained foot. It is still very weak.

5th Morning dull & threatening rain. Towards midday it cleared up. Four days without rain!

6th. Forenoon fair. Afternoon very wet. Had no school the last half of the day, as I had to settle accounts for the people. All assembled in Lachlan's house.

7th Through the night I was suddenly wakened by a terrible noise outside as if all the slates on the house rattled. It was a shower of rain or hail and such was the violence with which it beat against the house that at first I got a little frightened. Next day it was spoken of amongst the men as something unnatural. People cutting barley.

During my first year out on St Kilda I had a similar experience. I woke up in a great fright in the middle of the night, hearing a deafening staccato drumming and hissing across the flat roof of the building above me. It was a terrifying sound and like nothing I had ever heard before in my life. Waking from a deep sleep I thought we were being attacked. Then it stopped as abruptly as it had come and I realised it was a hail shower crossing the island with some force. I looked outside to see the ground white with hail the size of golf balls. The next morning at breakfast someone joked about the herds of wild buffalo galloping across the roof again in the night! Throughout the ensuing years I became used to being woken suddenly by such incidents, but it was still unnerving to hear as it would have been for George and the islanders.

Septr 8th Very wet and stormy. Evening turned out better.

9th Last night was very boisterous. Wet today again. By mid-day it turned out a terrible gale, which lasted till night. The sea was something to look at. The elements seemed at war with each other. Great damage done to crops. It was two days later in the season that the terrible storm prevailed last year.

All the people sick with the "cnatan" [cold].

This was known as the 'boat cold' and was the inevitable consequence of a visit by the steamers, passed on by the passengers. It totally incapacitated

THE KILN HOUSE
VILLAGE BAY.
ST. KILDA – FEB '08

the island population and indeed was quite a serious illness for them, having no mainland immunity to such things. Even to this day, any permanent staff getting off the helicopter on the island with a cold at the start of their month on were viewed with disfavour as we all knew it would go through everyone there.

10th Still wet & stormy, though nothing to what it was yesterday.

11th Strong gale blowing with heavy rain in forenoon. Evening turned dry. People cutting barley. I dressed Kate's foot. It looks better, though not getting much strength.

12th With the exception of a slight shower at midday, this day was clear & sunny.

13th Morning & forenoon fair. Shower in afternoon & also at 8pm. Men at Boreray for young gannets.

Septr 14th Beautiful day. Went with the men to Boreray, where I saw & took part in the slaughtering of the young gannets. It seemed to me barbarous work, but it is necessary to the existence of the St. Kildians. Finlay McQueen killed a puffin.

16th Yesterday & today other two excellent days. People busy at harvesting. Yesterday I helped a little at the scythe & today at stacking the barley.

Octr 1st From the 14th Ult. till today we had no rain except a slight shower early in the night of the 28th. We had not such a continuance of good weather all the summer at harvest as we have had during the last fortnight. On Thursday 23rd the people started cutting the crops & by Saturday night (25th) there was not a sheaf out on St. Kilda. I gave a hand to the most needful at stacking. At 11pm. of the 24th the "Robert Hadden" put into the bay. The men came on shore at 4am. next morning, when I got up to get news & read letters. Owing to contrary winds she was detained till the following Wednesday night. I spent the most of the time in writing and bidding Farewell to my friends in the world. I could not help feeling sad I could not get more news from home for the next eight or nine months. I trust, however, we may be all spared, if it is God's will, to meet again ere long, and if not here God grant that we may be prepared to meet on the other side of Jordan. Today several heavy showers of rain fell.

This would have been the last official boat out to the island. It was full of supplies for the islanders for the next eight months or so, as the gale season came upon them. Out on St Kilda during the first five years I was there, it seemed there was a definite pattern to the seasons. End of September and beginning of October, we were into 'Gale Alley' and gales continued till the end of November.

In December, curiously, we had spells of calm and mild almost spring-like weather, then January usually came roaring in with severe gales (one of the worst topped 148 miles an hour), snow and sleet and bitterly cold,

Hugh Murray, George's grandfather

Helen Murray (née Leslie), George's grandmother

John Murray, George's father

Jane Murray (née Ross), George's mother, with daughter Margaret

George's graduation

George Murray with schoolchildren, St Kilda, 1886–87

Katie MacAskill, 1891 (the date – 1896 – is when she was married.
In this photograph she is approximately 21)

George and Katie shortly after their marriage in 1896

Katie's mother

The Rev. Murdo MacAskill, Katie's father

This photograph has already appeared in 'Tarbat, Easter Ross,' by A. Fraser and F. Munro with the caption underneath, 'The Eviction from the Free Church Manse in 1906 of the Rev. George Murray, United Free Church minister and his family.' On the back of the photograph one of the family has written, 'Leaving the Manse at Tarbat, 1906'

Building the new U.F. church, Portmahomack, 1906 or 1907

Kilninver Free Church as it is today

Achnaluachrach house today

The house of Davochbeg as it is today

The old Kilninver Free Church and outlook circa early 1900s

Fulmar in Village Bay

Winter in Village Bay 1

Winter in Village Bay 2

Fulmars on the slopes of Oiseval

A summer's day in Village Bay

Soay sheep in Village Bay

A view through a Dun fissure

Summer on St Kilda

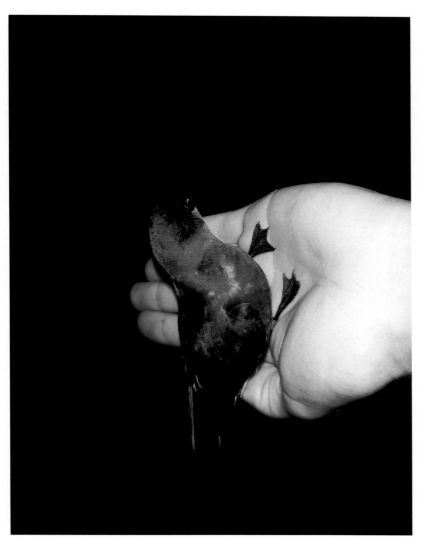

The European Storm Petrel, St Kilda (Photograph courtesy of Will Miles)

Cleits in Gleànn Mór

The street in January 2010

The street in winter sunshine

Dun from Mullach Sgar

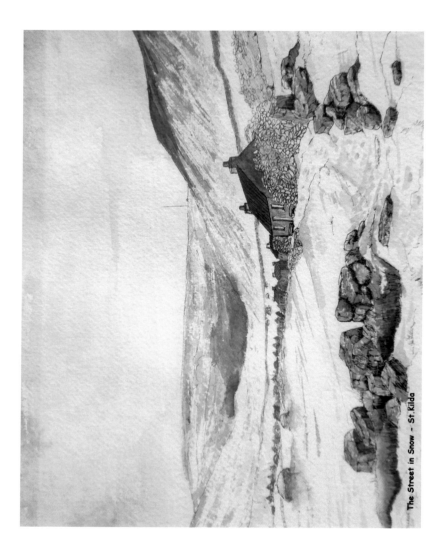

The Street in Snow - St.Kilda

The street in snow

The big cleit behind the manse

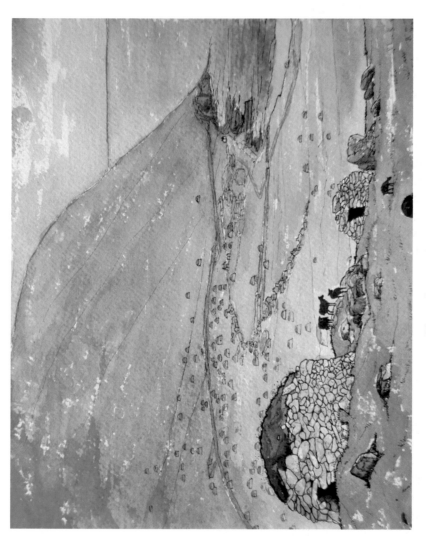

Cleits above Village Bay

as was February when snow usually arrived properly; either blown past on a fifty mile-an-hour gale or blanketing the island for a few days, or a week, then scoured away by bitter north-easterly winds. March was a mixture of rain, sleet and gales with occasional quiet days when the oystercatchers returned and set up their nesting territories, many over at Ruival among the tussocks of thrift that turned the area pink in May and June, the fulmars also came back to set up their territories. April was much of the same but now the puffins were returning, a small raft of them just below the gun and a few more of them each day. The weather now definitely felt warmer, days were longer and by the end of this month we could count on some good spells. May and June were usually the best and sometimes very warm and calm. In July we always had a gale of some sort and August was generally wet and midgy with horse flies a pest. September mostly good, but then … the gales once more.

Nowadays, the patterns no longer are the same and gales can strike at any time, even in May and June so yes, climate change seems to be upon us.

> *Octr 2nd Wet & misty. Forenoon spent in salting meat & putting past groceries etc. for the winter. On counting, I found that between Mrs McKinlay & myself there are to-day in the house 22lbs. tea, 96lbs. sugar, 2lbs. coffee & 2 tins of cocoa. We trust we may have health to consume it during the next nine months. In afternoon went up the village. Found my patient with the sprained foot going about the house. Returned early & read some of Miller's "My Schools & Schoolmasters".*

Hugh Miller was born in Cromarty in Easter Ross from a working class background and was educated at the local parish school, where he exhibited a love for the written word.

He was initially apprenticed as a stonemason and during this time became fascinated with the study of geology and fossils, going on to publish many works relating to these subjects. He was hugely prolific in other areas, publishing poems, Christian writings, local history and autobiographical works. He later became an accountant with a local bank and a well known personage. His death was tragic, as he shot himself in 1856, probably suffering, it is thought, from psychotic depression, which in Victorian times would have been difficult to diagnose let alone treat. He is today considered one of Scotland's premier palaeontologists and his descriptive prose has been recognised as being on a par with Thomas Hardy. His book of 'My schools and Schoolmasters' George obviously enjoyed hugely.

Octr 4th Yesterday (Sabbath) afternoon a south easterly gale came on with great fury & continued increasing till today. Through the night last night I actually thought the house would be blown down. Today the sea is grand to look upon. The waves come running against the gale and get their crests blown back for hundreds of yards. Heavy rain & occasional showers of hail accompanied the wind. Sheet lightning seen at night.

5th Gale still continues though not quite so boisterously. Towards evening it calmed down & presented a better & more settled appearance.

6th Mild & calm with occasional showers. In evening read some of Miller's. Now that the bustle with steamers etc. & writing is over I must set myself to reading & getting up Gaelic.

7th Got up at 7. After my Reading and prayer, I began Gaelic by reading Dr. McDonald's Gaelic poems. Very wet & misty.

Octr 1st Last night I found to my great surprise that I made a sad mistake in my reckoning for the last week, a mistake that is very apt to be made in a place of this nature. I cannot account for the mistake: When the "Robert Haddon" was here, I neglected my diary and on taking it up again I omitted a week, so that the dates of the previous week must be counted back a week.

Last night it blew a terrible gale and today on rising at 7 I beheld one of the grandest sights I ever saw. The sun shone brightly, the wind blew strongly from the S.E. and waves, running from twelve to fifteen feet

high, came right in to the bay and, dashing with tremendous force on the
shore & surrounding dykes, fell back again in one white sheet, as white
as the driven snow. This area of foam covering several acres, looked all
the more beautiful because the sun shone right down upon it. Not satisfied
with the view obtained from my window, I went to the shore & the sight
was one I shall never forget.

Octr 4th Saturday 2nd was a fine warm day with no rain. People cutting
hay.

Yesterday 3rd was misty with occasional slight showers. This is a bright
day, sky clear and very fine weather for the time of the year. A year back
from this date I was at home, having arrived on Saturday night after
four days tedious travelling from Loch Eport. Today I am surely far from
home out amid the wilds of the Atlantic; but I am thankful to God for
the greatest earthly blessing, my health. I am now four months here, and I
never once felt the hand of sickness approach me. Oh that I would praise
Him from Whom all blessings flow.

Octr 5th Very warm sunny day. No rain. Read some Gaelic & some of
Miller's with which I am greatly taken up. I like reading Gaelic well
enough, but soon get tired of it. As usual took my daily walk up the village.

6th Lay till 7.30 to-day. Must get up earlier as I lose much time in the
morning by lying too long when I might be reading to my advantage.
The atmosphere being so heavy here I have often to struggle hard against
sleep. The weekly prayer meeting being held tonight, I did not go up the
village. Occasional showers.

8th Yesterday (7th) was fair though threatening rain; to-day was much
the same. Very much overcast in afternoon. Sun presents an unusual red
appearance. No rain. Evening spent as usual in the village. This I do
all the oftener, as I am anxious to acquit myself in the speaking of the
Gaelic.

Octr 9th Very stormy. Strong wind & heavy rain. Sea running high. Stayed inside all day reading Gaelic & began Whewell's Moral Philosophy.

11th Yesterday (Sabbath) was mild and sunny with occasional showers. Was in church twice as usual, but I must confess that I make very little of the sermons I hear. It is poor feeding for the people or, rather, good food spoiled in the serving out.

Ecclesiastically matters are asleep.

Today wet & stormy. Heavy showers in the afternoon. After tea I went up the village to get the "Evening News". A deal of gossip floating at present, also rows in parts of the place. I take no side in the gossip. I listen and keep my opinions, as I have learned that, in St. Kilda as in many other places, "Silence is better than gold".

12th Occasional showers. Terrible shower of hail at 3pm. Read nothing to-day. Up the village in evening. People finished cutting grass & now the cattle are let inside the dyke. Fulmars now begin to return to the island.

The fulmar population came and went as they pleased, but they too had seasons of their own. In all the time I was there, I observed a distinct pattern in their movements. After nesting and rearing their young in the summer, they would drift off and by the end of September and the beginning of October only a handful was left to soar over the village and the hills. By the end of October and beginning of November, all were gone, the occasional small cluster appearing for a few days but never for long. Where did they go, I used to wonder? What other islands did they visit?

At Christmas time there was usually a small flock soaring around; they used to favour an area along from the gun where a small geo under the cliffs created great thermals. They'd launch themselves over it and use the updraught to take them out over the sea or up the steep cliffs and hill. They were always to be found playing in that spot. At the beginning of January they were gone again. But by the end of January/beginning of February quite a large flock would arrive to drift about the village. Then there would be another gap until the end of February/beginning of March saw them start to arrive back in earnest, with territories and serious nesting on their minds.

Fulmars, I discovered, mated for life and their time on this earth was around twenty – twenty-five years. There was a pair who returned year after year to nest in a cleit just outside the cookhouse window. We named them Mr and Mrs MacLeod and would anticipate their return every year. They came for eight years, and then the next year the cleit remained vacant. We decided that one of them had died, as one bird kept roosting there briefly then flying off again. It made us feel sad.

When I used to go out with my sketching equipment, I'd arrive at the chosen spot, set myself up and begin, only to have at least two or three of them floating by so close I could see in detail their curious bright eyes watching me and what I was doing. I had a favourite group of cleits I used to enjoy painting; above the quarry and halfway up the hill. Sitting there painting away, I'd hear the rush of wings and look up to see them whizzing past looking and looking. One had only one leg and became a favourite; he would soar past so close I could have reached out and touched him. They were intensely curious and I could be lying on the sheer edge of the Gap looking out to Boreray and the Stacs and there they'd be floating past watching and watching and oh, such effortless, fabulous fliers. If ever I have to be reincarnated as a bird it will be as a fulmar.

13th Octr Occasional slight showers with bright sun. In evening I cut down & salted a sheep I bought. I feel desperately sleepy these nights. Whenever it is ten o'clock I am overcome. I regret I do not get more reading done.

14th. Mild sunny day. No rain. Splendid weather for the season of the year.

Men, boys & some of the women had a great day at catching sheep. This lively & exciting work they call "Ruagadh", that is pursuing the sheep till they are caught in the chase. They caught a great many and on going up the village at night, I found in every house that they were busy slaughtering.

15th Strong wind. Pretty cold. No rain. Finished the reading of Miller's "Schools & Schoolmasters". He was certainly a very talented man. Read also part of Higgins' "Solar System".

When I started this project I actually located and bought a lot of the books he says he had for reading and further study, as I wanted to get a sense of the 'scholar' that he undoubtedly was. 'Higgins' Solar System' was definitely a scholarly read. Hopelessly out of date now, it would have been very informative in the 1880s. 'The Orbs of Heaven' was more metaphysical and thought provoking and obviously from his comments struck a few chords. I liked Miller's 'Schools and Schoolmasters', but hugely enjoyed Froude's 'Oceana'. James Froude was one of the foremost historians in Victorian England and 'Oceana' was about his travels in South Africa, Australasia and America. It became a best seller and would have been 'hot off the press', as it had been published in that year (1886). It was very readable.

16th Octr (Saturday) Occasional showers with breeze of wind. At 10.30am I set out for a walk going by Ruival, thence to the top of Scal [Mullach Sgar] and down the Brae. On arriving at the other end of the village I was informed that they were spending the day at "Ruagadh" the lambs and I set out with them, casting in my lot with D. McDonald & his boy. The first half of the day we spent after one mischief of a lamb which we at last got hold of. At 5P.M. we succeeded in getting other six on Ruival with the assistance of other two men. Had my dinner in D. McDonald's and arrived home at 6P.M. to meet , as I expected, an angry face on my landlady. I let the storm go past.

18th Yesterday was fair with a strong breeze of wind. Listened with more than usual attention to Mr. McKay's afternoon sermon.

Today strong wind. Occasional slight showers. Spent a few hours up the village.

19th Octr Slight rain in morning. Day cleared up well. Calm & mild for the season of the year. Men putting lambs onto the Dun and lifting potatoes. The potato crop is very poor, scarcely worth the trouble of lifting. At night I paid a visit to the manse. Was entertained kindly. I'll take people just as I get them; but I intend keeping clear of the gossip of the place as I cannot bear it.

20th Occasional slight showers. Calm & mild. Men at Boreray for sheep. One man brought home and killed a ewe sixteen years old. I was told that long ago, within the memory of the old people, they used to have sheep twenty years old.

21st Heavy showers through the day, also at 8.30 P.M. very wet. My landlady and a party in the village differed lately and today there was a great stir about alleged falsehoods on either side. May God keep [me] from all strife. I cannot bear it.

22nd Octr No rain. Calm & mild. Up the village in evening. One of the scholars is very ill with a pain in the head. The ground officer is also ill. After school I made a bow and arrow for one of the boys and in a few hours every [boy] in the village had one. Read little or nothing today.

23rd Beautiful warm morning. I am disposed to believe that it is much milder here at this season of the year than it is on the East Coast. This may be so for while frosts are now frequent on the mainland, we never feel any frost here yet. This morning I am told that few on the island saw such a night as there was last night. An old woman of eighty fighting with her daughter, a married woman. It came to blows. Others got entangled in the row, & a son of the old woman with his family left the house where he stayed with his mother. This was about midnight. It is terrible to think upon the like. She is a wicked old woman. May God in mercy visit her in her old age.

This has been a terrible day. After breakfast I went up the hill for a walk. I had not gone far when I saw the people removing furniture from one house to another. A family removed in consequence of the row. No sooner was this finished than another wicked woman began with her evil tongue speaking scandalous things about a married young man who she declared had something to do with herself. He flatly denies the charge laid against him. She is and has been a dangerous woman and yet I understand she is a great favourite at the manse. May God put down the evil that exists in our midst.

25th Yesterday was a beautiful day. It could not be more so in midsummer. Mr. McKay in his sermons made special reference to the disturbance amongst the people and prayed that the Lord would in mercy visit the old woman.

Today was somewhat dull and threatening rain. Such a continuance of calm settled weather was seldom seen at this season of the year in St. Kilda, though, I am told, they usually have good weather for a week or so towards the end of this month. Men were engaged dividing the grass amongst the rocks.

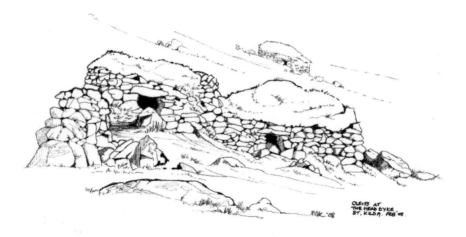

CLEITS AT
THE HEAD DYKE
ST. KILDA. FEB '08.

We have no idea what this means, perhaps to dry it out for hay for the livestock during the winter. The islanders were a fairly democratic society and their harvest of sea birds as well as fish catches were fairly divided out among the families on the Island.

From what transpired within the last few days and the reports current about certain persons in the island, one cannot help coming to the conclusion that morality is at low tide in St. Kilda. A great change for the worse has come over the island during the last thirty or forty years. No check to lawlessness.

Octr 27th Yesterday and today were dull days, but no rain. Turning cold. Did not go out this evening. Must devote more time to reading.

28th Forenoon fair but dark. Showers in afternoon. Had no school the latter part of the day as the scholars wanted leave to go for grass. Read for a few hours a book on astronomy, "The Orbs of Heaven". Very interesting. The mighty problems that such men as Copernicus, Kepler & Galileo grappled with show that they were men of great minds. Spent a few hours up the village.

30th Yesterday wet & misty. Today fair though dark. With D.McD I went round Osewall [Oiseval] for grass. Fulmars are now seen round the island. A young wife cut her hand badly. An old wife took ill with weakness in her limbs.

The nights are now getting long and I fear the superstition is beginning to move as the people tell me they hear something almost every night. Last Sabbath night several fled from their houses & went to the claeks [cleits] where their hay is stored & remained there till morning. A noise was heard out by Ruival, very likely rocks falling, and they never doubted that it was some enemy (Na Gaoill) bent on the destruction of the St. Kildians. The strange thing is that though I am out every night I never hear anything of the sort, nor do I expect to hear.

67

Novr 1st Winter has returned. Yesterday was fair with a strong breeze of wind which was accompanied by heavy rain at 8.30pm. A middle aged man suddenly took ill. He was found speechless lying in bed when they went home from church. It is some internal trouble. The Sabbaths I do not feel as I used. The preaching is dry and monotonous. The old man is doubtless at his best.

Very wet & stormy this evening. Went up the village. The oil in my lamp ran short & had to borrow a candle to take me home.

Novr 2nd High wind with rain. Sick people improving. Read little or nothing today. Went over the village at night.

3rd What a terrible night with wind last night. I really thought the window would be blown in. Today rain & wind. Prayer meeting in evening.

Gales were a regular occurrence at this time of year and in recent years as the climate changes they come any time! I remember us all sitting one evening in September watching something on the television in the VIP lounge, which had a huge picture window facing the bay, when a terrific gale began to blow up. It was blowing straight from the south and as one, our eyes slid towards the said window as it started to bow in alarmingly. In silence someone got up and closed the curtains and we vacated the room with alacrity, closing the door carefully behind us, making for the top rest room, which faced east, to finish watching our programme.

Our office window was regularly blown in. It was in a corner of one of the buildings and seemed to attract swirls of wind usually accompanied by stones picked up along the way! After about the third or fourth time of this happening a sheet of high density perspex was affixed to its front, preventing any further accidents. It is now rather battered and dented but has served its purpose well!

While we are on the subject of gales; we have survived some of terrifying ferocity. The worst were usually in early January and I was out on St Kilda during the time of the great storm which struck Uist and the rest of the Western Isles in early January 2005. This one resulted in the tragic loss of an entire family on South Uist; a mother, father, grandfather and two small children, as they tried to get to safety on that terrible night.

On St Kilda, as a military base, we always got the latest weather reports and particularly any adverse weather coming our way. I and the rest of the crew change going out from Benbecula after the New Year that January, had been delayed getting to the island by bad weather; gales and rain battering the islands for about a week. We finally made an attempt on the seventh day and set off in fairly windy conditions, but by the time we got out as far as the Monach Islands, we were being flung around the sky, the small Dauphin helicopter dropping like a stone in some of the wind's troughs. I remember the pilot looking round at us all, some of us white faced and wryly asking if we should go back. None of us could speak, but we nodded a yes, very emphatically. We set off again the following day in a rising gale blowing from the east. Easterlies were good winds for the pilots; straight into the bay and no turbulence once there. The timing to get us in and out that day was tight. The weather was deteriorating, the rising wind due to shift round to the west later with severe gales forecast. It was a now or never situation, every one conscious that the crew waiting to come off had been there over their allotted time and wanted HOME.

We were loaded up with all our baggage and as many ration supplies as we could carry and, assisted by the straight easterly, we made it to St Kilda in record time. Flying over Levenish, round Oiseval and into the village area, we all noticed that the stream that fed the dam near the helipad was being blown, along with the water spilling over the dam edge, straight up into the air and back towards the hill. Not a good sign we thought. It took more than a few minutes to actually put down on the helipad; ourselves and the contents of the chopper were speedily unloaded, a quick handover with the outgoing crew and they were off out of the bay, wobbling over Levenish, the huge rock at the entrance, then they were lost to sight.

All personnel were now safely in the base but the weather report looked grim; strengthening winds reaching in excess of 120 miles an hour and we all knew what that meant; 120mph and add another twenty on for St Kilda. Plans were made at an impromptu meeting in the Puffinn, as the wind began to shift round to the south and west. The maintenance staff would check on the generators in the power station and then all other checks were to be suspended and no one was to leave the buildings until the gale had abated. We went round checking all doors and windows were secured and all curtains closed to minimise any damage caused by windows shattering. The afternoon wore on and darkness began to fall. I got dinner underway, hoping the generators wouldn't break down and then we all settled in for a night in the Puffinn, the safest place to be in the middle of the complex, to wait it out. The noise by this time was indescribable and the roaring of the wind and occasional debris hitting the roof was so loud we had to shout to make ourselves heard. The flat roofs of the base had a thick layer of bitumen with small stones embedded in it. These stones started to come loose with the force of the wind and began coming down the ventilation shafts, one of which was situated in the middle of the bar. After a few stones had pinged off a few glasses, we all moved over a bit as a small pile began to form under it. At about ten o'clock the rain began in earnest, battering all round the base and the nurse and I went off to make sandwiches and tea for everyone. At one in the morning, some decided to just go to bed and hope for the best. A few minutes later they were back at the gallop. Two windows had blown in in the manse accommodation, and there was a river running into the Sergeants' Mess sitting room from a broken window at the top of the room.

The rain water had been pouring off the hillside and had become channelled round the kitchen block and into the U-shaped gap above the sitting room; with inadequate drainage, nowhere to go and finding a broken window, it had rushed in. The maintenance staff managed to batter a hole in the outside wall leading to the beach and out the water rushed. We now had a small river running through the room, but hey, it would stop eventually. A trail of refugees made their way, with their bedding and personal effects, from the ruins up to the top corridor and the spare rooms. Around half past two in the morning the wind began to ease slightly, not that we could really tell the difference, but at any rate, the rest of us decided to go off to bed and try to sleep.

The next day the wind had died down a lot and we took stock of the damage. The generators, which miraculously had kept running, were checked and we marvelled at the sight that greeted us. Boulders the size of fridges had been deposited on the road a good twenty feet up from the shore. Slates from the manse, church and Factor's house roofs were everywhere, sliced forcefully into the turf. Stones littered the place and several cleits and chunks of the head dyke wall were down. The helipad was buried deep in a thick layer of rocks and debris from the shore and strange long strips of turf and vegetation had been torn up. We discovered later that these had been caused by twisters within the gale and they had also affected the Uists, in that some houses had lost entire gable ends, while houses next door were intact. Certain roofs were totally stripped of slates while others remained untouched.

Inside the base, there were two windows in the manse accommodation blown in, several broken along the front, the office window had come in and there was a pile of small stones in the base at the foot of every ventilation shaft; we crunched over the mound in the laundry room. The Sergeants' Mess sitting room was a sodden mess with a large hole in the front wall! During the rash of phone calls from the Uist side to see if we were still there and all right, we heard of the tragedy and grieved for the families while we set to clearing up, thankful that there had been nothing but a few broken windows and a flood.

The sheep flock had taken refuge in the cleits, as they usually did when a storm hit. We saw them streaming in single file back out of their stone shelters. They had their favourites and had an uncanny way of predicting just when a storm would strike. I remember once, deep down in Gleànn Mór, sitting behind a group of large stones out of the wind obliviously sketching away, when I became aware of a line of sheep making their way with great speed down the hill towards the shelter of the old settlement. The sky was still clear and nothing seemed out of the ordinary, but I packed everything up just in case and headed up on the long slog out of the glen.

THE FAIRY HOUSE
VILLAGE BAY - ST. KILDA . MAR.'08

MK.

Before I'd got a quarter way down the hill on the other side, towards the base, the sky darkened and the wind began to blow in sheets of freezing rain from the south-west. I was soaked to the skin when I got back but would have been even colder, wetter and more miserable had I not paid attention to what was going on with the sheep.

We had many such gales. Another memorable one was in January of 2009. There were high winds forecast, but nothing, we thought, out of the ordinary. Well, ordinary to us out there. Then, sometime around 12.30 am on that Saturday night, the wind struck the front of the VIP block with great force and peeled back the front ridge of the roof like a sardine can, the wind hurling debris and large bits of concrete block into the rooms all along its length.

Harry, one of the technicians, later remarked with typical Glasgow humour that there he was, reading his exciting sci-fi novel in bed, when he became aware that the meteorite shower bombarding the space ship was in fact landing around him on the bed! There was another trail of refugees clutching bedding that night, making their way up to the top corridor and safety. Then it was noticed in the headcount that Ewan, the kitchen assistant, whose room was down there, was missing. On entering his room fearing the worst, they found him fast asleep, hand cradling his cheek, totally oblivious to the world, debris all around him and his bed.

Next morning the resulting mess was predictable. The office window had come in again, all the bedrooms in the VIP block were damaged and the VIP lounge had large pieces of concrete reclining on the settees and carpet. The roof had rolled itself back down again, but the gusty wind was still blowing and there were ominous thumping noises coming from it. Two dining room windows had been broken and we discovered that gusts had reached 135 miles an hour over the island. High winds are a most frightening thing to hear.

George would not have encountered the like before and would have been suitably alarmed.

4th Occasional showers. Monthly prayer meeting. Read at night some Gaelic poems.

6th Yesterday wind & rain. Removed books, desk &c from church to the house as the church is now getting very cold. Today wind and rain. Was on Mullach Scal. [Sgar] Pretty cold At night had some showers of snow.

9th Last three days wind & rain with occasional showers of hail. Pretty cold. Today thanksgiving day. Woman hurt her foot yesterday. Two of the scholars ill also. Old man ill with rheumatism & head

Novr 11th Yesterday & today wind and rain, cold. Tonight I started a Singing School with the children. I intend holding it once a week to learn them some tunes. Read very little this week.

15th Friday was fair and not so cold. People were after the poor sheep – those that they do not expect to live, they take home & kill. I went as far as the Camber [Cambir] and took home a sheep a good part of the way for a woman who was not very strong.

Saturday was showery. Men went to Boreray. They saw one young gannet & two young puffins. I read the most of the day & finished the "Orbs of Heaven". I became lost in amazement on reading that the nearest fixed stars are so far distant that light, travelling at the rate of 12,000,000 miles per minute, takes 1,000 years to reach us.

Yesterday was wet & misty.

An old woman & one of the scholars ill yesterday. I intend taking a note at the end of this book of all the illnesses that occur amongst them, taking the names of the patients, as it may yet be beneficial in a place where there is no medical aid. Today very wet.

Novr 16th Wind & snow. Tops of hills white for the first time this season. Am reading Froude's "Oceana".

17th Occasional heavy showers of rain. Find "Oceana" very interesting. Spent the latter part of the night in the manse. Found them kind and I must take everyone as I find them and not believe all I hear.

19th Very wet yesterday. Did not go out. Today wet & misty. Am troubled about a family who are not sending peats to the school as they ought. They are bent on nothing but a row. I do nothing rashly and gave them a fair chance by showing kindness to their children, thus trying to induce them to send them and so preserve peace; but if this does not have any effect by the beginning of the week I must take other steps.

It was the tradition in many parts of the Highlands to have each pupil bring a peat from home every day, to help feed the fire in the school room. Perhaps George introduced the custom to St Kilda, as I can find no other record of it being commonplace.

Novr 20th Wet in forenoon. Not so cold. Stir in village to-day again about alleged lies & theft. Really it is a terrible place and Satan seems to

have a few strongholds on the island. May God destroy them. O God set
a watch at the door of my lips and keep me out of all strife.

24ᵗʰ Last four days wet & misty; but not stormy or cold. Place in a
stir as usual. I am very glad I got over the peat difficulty in peace with
exercising patience. Still reading "Froude" but I spend a deal of time
out. I improved greatly in my Gaelic since I came to the island. For the
last fortnight there is a gull of a rare species on the island. I never saw
one of them before. It is about the size of the Blackbacked Gull, perhaps
thicker in the body & neck. Not any of it is pure white, but dark greyish
like a white bird covered with mud. It is mostly all of the same colour,
the head, about the eyes, being the darkest. Bill is nearly white &, if I
mistake not, black on the point. The back is mottled. It approaches very
near to the houses.

This would have been a Glaucous Gull and would probably have been a young adult in its first year. Glaucous gulls are a northern species from the Arctic, common down through the Faroes and Iceland and they are sometimes seen in coastal waters in the north-west of Scotland in the winter months. We used to have the odd one or two appear in November and December on St Kilda; as large as a black-backed gull and very bold in their manner. They are scavengers, preying on carrion, eggs, chicks and anything at all edible.

In June on Svalbard, when I was there a few years ago, they were everywhere, very watchful for the least sign of a food opportunity and I remember feeling anguished and helpless as I watched two of them drive off a pair of Barnacle geese from their nest on a cliff face, returning to gobble up all their eggs. Poor poor geese, all that way thousands of miles up from Scotland and Ireland to breed and now – nothing.

I was told they would not lay again that year, all their energy had been expended in the long migratory flight to Spitsbergen, making their nest and producing their eggs. The nesting season is so short up there that even if they did, the chicks, if they survived, would not fledge in time to make the long journey south for the winter. While I was there in the Arctic, on a remote peninsula on the west, I watched an Arctic fox one morning quartering a site of nesting terns and gobbling up chicks and eggs. I was reminded that in the high Arctic everything has to eat to survive, foxes and Glaucous gulls included, but oh, I felt so distressed for the geese and the poor terns.

Novr 27th Last three days calm & warm, though occasionally wet. I'm told that for the last twelve years, the month of November was not so mild and free from gales. Today being Saturday I set off to the Camber, where I fell in with a young girl who told me she was putting the sheep and rams together. Things would look better and leave a better impression upon a stranger, were the fair sex to leave these things to the opposite sex. On returning to the village I was put out not a little by several people putting questions to me about the sheep – questions that I little looked for, expected and much less wished for. There is a great want of modesty still clinging to the rocks of St. Kilda. Men shifting sheep on the rocks.

Novr 29th Yesterday and to-day stormy. Showers of hail. Yesterday there was a baptism in church, John McDonald, about sixteen months old. I know not why he was so long without being baptized. Ceremony pretty long, forming in fact a short sermon.

There is much talk at present about the conduct of the minister towards a member of the church, L.M. This member speaking about a <u>bad woman</u> in the village said "he would rather she was in the middle of the sea, but that she is yet in the land of mercy." For this he is shut out from the privileges of the church for the time being. I am careful not in any way to interfere between parties; but my opinion is that the minister acted more upon the suggestion of others than according to just judgement. The woman is certainly bad and has often been the cause of scandalous noise in the village; and yet is a favourite at the manse; that is [what] provokes the people and doubtless strengthens the workers of iniquity. I have repeatedly heard from members of the church that it is far from *being right, and what is more I am told that the minister will not now pass the said member's house.*

Decr 1st Yesterday was cold with showers of hail. Spent part of last night in the manse. The stir these days is that the precentor in the church was seen several times to laugh on Sabbaths and they are threatening dethronement. His confession was that he was made to laugh when the steamers were coming here by some of the people (natives) eating sweets in a curious manner. Most laughable. A terrible wild night last night. Today the hills are white with December blasts.

Decr 2nd Last night war was waged between D.F. Elder and myself about the peats to which I formerly referred. As the boys persisted in not bringing them I could stand it no longer and after dismissing the school I spoke to them and asked the reason. Not getting a satisfactory reply I called later on at the house and met the elder in a most furious rage about speaking to <u>his</u> boys about peats. He began with something I did not take up about fellow countrymen in Cataoibh (Sutherland), I told him to take it easy, that there was no reason for all the raving madness. He accused me of falsehood and is the first man that accused me of such. I closed him at last, for his wife had to admit that they were not bringing the required number of peats at first, but how long it continued she could not tell. Further, she said that none ever hindered the boys from bringing the peats. I question that very much, for to one of the other scholars she said one day "You fool, bringing peats to the schoolhouse (tighmhor)". Though I triumphed, I was put about and slept very little. Sad to think how a man in his position delights in rows for no cause. May God uphold me in this place. Today quite white with snow. Hard frost last night.

Decr 4th I am not yet the better of the trouble I got with the Elder. Never did any man trouble me more and that without a cause. He did not come yet to ask forgiveness for the way he used me and till he does so I'll keep at my distance, nor do I think I do wrong in so doing. I intend keeping my

77

own place and not lower it for him. It is hard to think that a person far away from friends should be thus treated by one who ought to be a source of comfort and advice.

Today fine. Wet at night.

Decr 7ᵗʰ Weather cold with showers of snow for the last few days. Wind north. Island fairly quiet at present. Read very little lately.

Decr 8ᵗʰ Great storm. Morning snow and wind. Towards mid-day turned to rain. Wind very high at night. Terrible sea on. Pity those on the sea. Spent a few hours in manse. Am reading Cowper's "Task".

Decr 9ᵗʰ The storm continued till about 1.30 this morning, at which time I went to bed. Very seldom has such high wind been heard. Several stone dykes fell and one house was almost roofed.

11ᵗʰ Weather settled. Reading "Disruption Worthies". I am enjoying my food now better than I was for the last ten days. I must endeavour not to be troubled by small quarrels.

13ᵗʰ Yesterday & today fair but cold. Mr. McKay preached much better yesterday than usual. His subject was the Prodigal Son.

Decr 14ᵗʰ Today cold but dry. A shower of hail. This morning at 0.30am was born ------------ McKinnon. Parents Neil and Mrs. McKinnon. Child large and very promising. Mother doing well.

16ᵗʰ Still cold, with snow on hills. Last night for the first time since we disagreed I saw the Elder in Lachlan's. No words were exchanged between us. It is the first time that I ever passed by anyone without a word. I still maintain, and so do others, that he ought not to do as he did, but he is above acknowledging that.

PUFFINS – ST. KILDA
VILLAGE BAY

18th Great snow storm. Hard frost. Very high wind last night. Today also much drifting. Stayed in all day reading Dr. Wolff's travels. Must devote more time to the reading of the Bible in English and Gaelic.

20th A deal of snow fell early yesterday (Sabbath) morning. Fair during the day. Heard the minister read a few verses out of the Old Testament for the first time since I came -- a few verses out of Ezekiel. Should he not read the O.T. oftener? Today still hard frost with showers of snow. St. Kilda looks well when covered with snow. The people in single file carrying home peats over the white hills presents a curious spectacle.

Decr 22ⁿᵈ Yesterday was very wet. Mostly all the snow has disappeared. The child that was born a week ago took ill, the jaws fell last night and it is not expected to live long. It certainly is something very wonderful for it got all the attendance that could be bestowed upon it.

24ᵗʰ Showers of snow again. Time is passing, the day no longer gets shorter. Must be at work. Child still struggling between life & death. It is surprising how it stands it so long.

Decr 25ᵗʰ. Christmas day. Forenoon snowing heavily. It being Saturday I wished to exercise my limbs by taking a walk, for the 'New Style' is not kept in St. Kilda and so there was nothing out of the usual routine to take place. On reaching the tops of the hills it was just the thing for a Christmas – heavy flakes of snow falling fast and thick, while all around was already white and the small hamlet below seemed asleep under the thick atmosphere.

What a contrast to the stir and bustle of a town on such a day as this. I continued my journey till I reached the "Carnmhor", where I fell in with four men who had gone out for peats and with whom I returned. Connacher, the highest hill, had by this time presented a peculiar appearance. In shape it is conical, just as the extinguished volcano had, in ages gone past, left it. The snow was now blowing off the very top and was carried away in a cloud. One would almost fancy that volcanic eruptions were beginning to intrude on our small desolate empire.

I cannot help reflecting upon the way and place I used to spend my Xmas holidays – in Ballater with my friends, how happy. This year I cannot as much as hear whether all my friends are spared to enjoy this season of the year as happily as usual. Now my thoughts turn homewards. How are they? May God bless them and all those who contributed to my happiness when with them. My fellow students – some of them have gone to rest in the grave, others enjoying the Christmas feast at home, and I am here.

O how thankful I ought to be for the blessing of health God has been pleased to bestow upon me, not a single day ill since I came here more than six months ago.

In 'Old Calendar' reckoning, Christmas day fell on January 6th, while New Year's Day fell on the 14th January.

Decr 27th Yesterday cold with heavy showers of hail. Mr. McKay preached yesterday again twice upon the Prodigal Son, that being the third Sabbath and the sixth sermon on the same subject.

Today very wet and stormy. Last night at 10.30 the child, after six days intense suffering, departed this life. Everyone expressed great wonder how it lived so long after being seized with illness, as they generally succumb at the end of a week after they are born. This one was thirteen days except 1 1/2 hours. It had a frequent cry since it was born; but the first sign of its being dangerously ill was at the end of a week, when it ceased to suck the breast, but still sucked the bottle. The following day "thuit na gialan" (the jaws fell), when all hope of its recovery was given up. From that time till its death it occasionally took a little milk in a spoon or out of the bottle. The last two days a little wine in water was given once or twice. It very often yawed [the dictionary meaning of "yawed" is taken from a shipping term and one of the explanations is 'to deviate from a course, or move to and fro'. Perhaps he means the infant moved or writhed to and fro in an effort to find relief] *and sometimes looked hard at you.*

It was pitiful to see the poor little thing in the pangs of death. May God prepare us all for the same end. In the grave which was opened I saw the coffins of its two little brothers that died the same way. The one coffin was still quite whole, there being only about sixteen months since it was interred; the other was in pieces. I sympathize with the parents in their bereavement. I think something should be done to endeavour to lessen the plague. Want of attendance and care at the time of birth was lately held out as the cause. This, in its turn, like all the other supposed causes, must be abandoned, for I can honestly say that both the nurse and the parents did all in their power to keep at bay the "dreaded plague". It is not for me to say what the long sought for cause is, but, as one without any skill whatever, I would attribute it to the work of the women, and partly, perhaps, to their too frequent exposure to the cold owing to their being barefoot, more than to anything else.

1887

Jany 1ˢᵗ Another year has run its course. How good the Lord has been to me. I know not that I was as much as one day ill during the year that has just expired.

'New Year's day' in St. Kilda is not held in the new reckoning so that this day was in no way different from others. The men had the lines set last night for ling and this morning they went to lift them. The shore was not a very pleasing sight when they went out; but by the time they got back, there was a terrible swell on and really it was a job to get them landed. Every one that was able to walk was at the shore assisting as best they could. I thought several times that the boat would be swamped with them amongst the breakers or dashed on the rocks. First the lines, fish & oars were landed by means of ropes, then, when all on the shore were ready to pull and an opportunity was afforded by the waves, the nine men in the boat held fast clinging to the sides and let it run with the wave on the rocks. The united effort of all of us on the shore, hauled it right up clear out of the water. It was neatly done without any damage except that one woman was knocked down and slightly run over. The girls afterwards told me that they thought I was to faint as I stood looking at the men in danger, so pale did I look. I was anxious indeed, but I felt no fear or weakness coming on me as they said. Really it is a dangerous shore. They got about twenty ling and as many yesterday. That is how I spent the 1ˢᵗ Jany 1887. Have now written a letter to Father. It may be that we will see a vessel passing soon to which we may have access. How I wish we would.

Jany 4th Snow, heavy snow yesterday and very cold. On Sabbath last we had the 7th & 8th sermons on the Prodigal Son. Minister pretty brisk in the afternoon.

Last night I heard that the Elder, with whom I had the dispute lately, is watching me like a tiger for his prey. Tomorrow the Xmas prizes are to be distributed amongst the scholars and if his children do not get what he thinks proper, I will get a "supper" (ie. I will get from his tongue what will suffice for a supper). He did not spare the other two, the latter of whom he brought to tears with his language. [This would have been Hugh McCallum] *Of this he boasts. Poor man, I'm sorry for him. Should he commence on me, which he very likely will, I am resolved not to open my mouth and so silence him with silence. I have conscientiously awarded the prizes to the deserving parties and I care not should he or any other roar about them till the rocks tire of echoing. I am sorry indeed to see that such a man is an elder in a Church. Went today to the top of Conagher. Knee depth snow there.*

Jany 5th 12 o'clock. Xmas day here. Distributed the prizes amongst the scholars and gave them play for ten days. Very heavy rain last night and this morning.

Jany 10th Thursday & Friday were spent in exercising my limbs on the hills. On Saturday we set out to Soa for sheep for the New Year Feast. Starting at eleven o'clock (much too late) we encountered a heavy sea when doubling "Gob an Dun" and were on the point of retracing our steps, when we saw that the sea ahead of us did not present quite such a formidable appearance as we anticipated. After two hours' hard rowing we reached Soa, where we landed, not without great difficulty, on steep rocks which we had to climb. Three were left in charge of the boat. From the landing place to the top of Soa I took close on half an hour climbing, so steep was it.

The day by this time was beautiful and warm and glad was I to find plenty snow to quench my thirst. The top of the island is a flat covered with long strong grass. It is on this flat that the St. Kildian Olympiads take place annually in Autumn and Winter. Before I reached the top they had already caught and bound four sheep in the first onset. All the sheep had now disappeared down amongst the rocks and whilst one man goes down and drives them up, the others are distributed over the flat with the dogs at their sides. We were just an hour and a half on land and in that time we caught twenty. The best of it was yet to come. From the top we had to carry them now down the steep to the boat, two sheep per man. I and one of the scholars, not being accustomed to heavy burdens, got ours on ropes on each end and slid them down the best way we could, now dragging them after us, now letting them down before us over precipices till we reached. It was now getting dark, but the moon just began to peep round St. Kilda Proper.

On reaching the shore where the men were assembled lading the boat, I found myself on a rock about forty or fifty feet above the water on which the boat was heaving like a bird. Words and hesitation were out of place at the time, so without a word I tied a rope about my middle and waited orders.

"There," said the man at the top," Fix your hands and your feet on the rope that I hold and let yourself slide down." Without a moment's hesitation I acted upon the injunction and the next moment found me safely in the boat. Thus were all the men and the sheep got in. As for the dogs, poor brutes, they had to fare worse, being thrown out into the sea they swam to the boat and were picked up. By this time a breeze got up and fears were entertained that we would have to spend the night in the boat as the sea must at this time have been running very high at "Gob an Dun" and to attempt through the 'Caolas' between Dun and the mainland by night was to say the least of it a great risk. The wind being favourable as we returned at the end of an hour we reached the Caolas where some cried "Go on", while others cried "No that nothing but death was before us". In such a boiling and foaming place not twenty yards wide, there was cause for fear. On we went and came out on the other

*side safely, thus saving about two hours hard rowing should we get round
the cape. I got home at 7.30 P.M. after a most adventursome day, pretty
hungry, of course, for though we took provisions, we had no time to wait
to eat them nor indeed could we very well for we were wet and cold. Thus
I spent one of my Xmas holidays in St. Kilda.*

I have been through the gap in Dun once in our fast rib at high tide and
we went from the shelter and calmness of the bay through it into a fierce
swell and high choppy waves on the other side. The only way we would
ever have attempted it at all was at high tide, as there are submerged rocks
in the channel at other times. Hundreds of years ago, the headland of Dun
was joined to the main island of Hirta with an arch but this fell into the sea
leaving this gap. The island has always suffered from rock falls. We used
to hear them sometimes from the base and one day the nurse and I had
just returned from a walk up the hill when we heard a dull thump and roar
towards Ruival and looking over saw that a large part of the cliff face was no
longer there, but had descended into the sea. A sobering thought.

*Yesterday was a very fine day. In the forenoon we heard the 9th Sermon
on the Prodigal Son. In the afternoon for the first time since I came a
chapter was read and a sermon preached out of the Old Testament (Hos
XIV.1). Not a bad sermon at all; but most of us were taken aback as we
had no Bibles but Testaments. It was about time that the Prodigal Son
was left and something given out of the Old Testament. Today bright
with a stiff breeze. At this season of the year my thoughts naturally tend
homewards. Thank God I am in full enjoyment of health and strength. I
am reading Sir W. Hamilton's Lectures on Metaphysics.*

*Jany 17th Past week pretty wet and stormy. Yesterday morning very wild
with wind and rain. Minister's text from John 111.16 .*

*A terrible storm arose at midnight last night and still (10 am.) continues
high wind and rain. The bay is one mass of foaming water – waves
rolling high and the salt spray driven I'm sure half a mile inland.*

Jany 19th Was last night out for a few hours and from what I heard, there are two families watching every movement I make – in school, - outside - and inside – to see if they can get anything to speak about. O Lord do thou enable me so to walk that I need not be ashamed who sees my actions and hears my words. I wish them no ill nor did I do any harm to them.

Weather cold with hail occasionally.

20th A stiff cold breeze. Had the Singing Class at night. Learned them Boylston a short measure tune. They quickly pick up the tunes. Also started them with the hymn "I love to think of the Heavenly Land". God grant that it may be blessed to them.

Jany 21st Still blowy with mist & rain. Spent a few hours in the manse at night, where I was told that that extraordinary elder (D.F.) who troubled me so much, had been giving the minister a <u>doing up</u> for

something he said on Wednesday at the prayer meeting and which the elder took to himself. It was enough to raise him and he declared Satan must have gone into the minister either when he (the elder) was engaged in prayer or when we were singing. Suffice it to say that he went that night at eleven o'clock in a terrible rage demanding an explanation, where he was told that the words were addressed to the congregation. I thought to myself that "if the coat suits him he may by all means put it on" and be none the worse. Really he is a terrible man – yes terrible and dangerous. Strong words to use about any elder.

Things haven't changed much over the years. Rows around the place unfortunately, were even familiar to me when I was out on St Kilda. Although the numbers of people out on the Island fluctuated in the summer months, in the winter there was only us on the base, usually around twelve to fourteen personnel. We saw each other every day, had meals together and also socialised with each other for the whole of our month on duty. We were together for most of the time. It was essential therefore, that we all got on. There were inevitable clashes of personalities and they were dealt with, usually with an apology from each party and a handshake, but some spats were indeed of a serious nature. It was difficult in an environment as remote as St Kilda to maintain cordial relations at all times, especially with some personnel you would not normally have chosen to have as a friend.

It was always worst just after New Year. In midwinter it got light at around half past nine in the morning, the darkness coming down again at about quarter to three in the afternoon. Less than six hours of daylight and it seemed to act as a trigger for any potential skirmishes. We usually had at least one major bust up and row during that time. Like George, I tried to keep out of any skirmishes and retired to my room at speed if things threatened to get out of hand. It was, as I said, usually short lived and then February arrived, with some longer days and the promise of spring and things quietened down again for another year.

Jany 25th Wet and stormy these days. Wind high S.E.

28th This is really an extraordinary place. The wild man above us who flitted from another house in the end of harvest owing to the rows, was just on the point of coming down to us Monday night to see what noise were we making. The minister's servant was in with us and the only noise was talking and breaking coals.

Feby 4th May God preserve me, for I was never in such a state.

The row above referred has become serious. On the afternoon of Jany 31st I went to the manse and were talking over the business when Mrs. Gillies, who stays above us, came in. She there maintained strongly before us that there [was] something unusual in our kitchen on the Monday night referred to. The minister's servant said there was not. I told her that she had not the truth and so should be quiet and that it was as great a lie as ever a man made. She marched out and on going she told her husband that I lifted my hand to her face. O God pardon her for thou knowest I did not do so. I was not in (at home) five minutes when "the man" (an duine glas), as he is called, came to the door and accused me of abusing his wife in the manse, that I lifted my hand to her and will (he affirmed) doubtless be the cause of her death. Of course I flatly denied the accusation and told him that I told her nothing but the truth and that she now told another and a worse lie in saying that I lifted my hand to her face. That set his blood aboiling and a scene followed. I received terrible abuse from that man and expected once or twice to have his stick drawn across my face. He swore, told me I had no character and that nothing but poverty brought me here. I spoke loudly, but took good care what I said. The farthest I went was in saying that though she would cry for ten years I could not help it as I just told her the truth. I wished him to go to the manse, where I had three witnesses that I did not lift my hand to her. He simply replied that he would not take the minister for a witness.

He declared he would be at law with me and the last words he said was that he would meet me yet.

That night I did not go to bed, but sat up having the biggest of the schoolboys along with me. There is [no] saying what that man might do when he is in a passion as he said about a month ago when rowing with others, that if he were well there would be plenty coffins tomorrow. He is an extraordinary man. May God have mercy upon his soul. On another occasion when rowing he was heard to say that he twisted many a man's neck and he seemed to delight, I'm told, in telling how he used to kill the black people in foreign countries. Is there any wonder that I would be afraid to go to bed.

Next night I kept the lamp lighted and slept pretty well, being rather tired. Last night I put out the lamp, but slept very little, having started up several times on hearing the storm, I suppose. Another time I must have dreamt that I heard somebody at the door as I got up in the bed and listened and was going to call out 'who is there' when I thought it was most likely a dream.

This is a terrible place. O God in mercy visit it.

She is still lying, I'm told, whether she is sick or not.

Feby 7th The results of the row have become still more serious. In one family the wife was taking the part of Gillies & the wife, and the man was on the minister's & mine. It reached such a pitch that she left the house and went to her father's on Friday with the two children and is still (Monday) there. The husband is brother to the minister's servant. Their father, who was also in the house, is staying in the manse. Things were not in such a state of matters for many, many a year.

Feby 9th Last night D.F. the Elder made peace between the husband and wife and I expected we were to enjoy peace for some time; but this evening, after the prayer meeting, the same elder came in and told me that he is out on the minister through the servant and that he does not intend going to Church unless he put away the servant if she does not go and speak to him (Elder) at his house.

May God in mercy visit our island for really it looks as if Satan were gaining ground daily.

How can we expect a blessing where there is such continual strife?

The Elder might very well, I think, have let this past for such a trifle if I am properly informed; but on the other hand there is certainly too much gossip carried into & conducted in the manse. That I cannot deny. Kind as they are to me I must speak the truth.

I commenced revising some mathematics; but do very little owing to the state of matters. Weather fair & good.

19ᵗʰ I am really ashamed to begin writing again about rows.

Last Wednesday night again after the prayer meeting, there was a scene in the manse, owing to a member of the church saying; on being asked why the elder was keeping away from the church, among other things, that there was too much gossip going on in the manse. Certainly he is not wrong there. This made a terrible noise and the servant went at once to where the Elder was and asked what he had against her. He told her that he had nothing against her but against the minister. How he reconciles that statement with what he told me is rather difficult for me to see. Next day the minister went to his house and, with difficulty, I understand, came to an understanding. The elder is now going again to church after absenting himself and all his family one Sabbath and one prayer meeting evening. To what understanding they came I know not. O God, may peace and love exist amongst us, especially with respect to church matters. Strife and discord are far too prevalent amongst this small community. Why are thy blessings restrained from us but because of our iniquities. Keep me, O Lord, in the way to Zion. May I be meek, patient, bearing a hatred to all strife.

Feby 22ⁿᵈ How busy Satan is amongst us! Alas that it should be so on an island that saw a very good day from the Lord.

The above mentioned row was settled Thursday. On Friday matters were ripening for another, which burst forth early Saturday morning. It happened thus. A young girl who frequented the manse, received great kindness there, and who stayed in it for at least a twelvemonth, had on Xmas afternoon, it was said, carried away from the manse a few words which the servant said about the much-spoken-about Elder, and told it to another family. As is the fashion whenever a row starts, everything is raked up and this was with everything else. The servant denies that ever she said the words and the other denies that ever she said such a thing against the servant, & this she asserts in the face of three witnesses who affirm that she did. This stir was carried on, I understand, till midnight on Saturday. The girl is expelled from the Sabbath School. This is supposed to serve as a check and I believe it does. It is looked upon as a great privilege deprived from them for some time, though I must confess that it seemed very absurd to expel from the Sabbath the very persons who have most need to be taken in.

When any one reads about all these rows, one cannot help noticing how often that Elder and the minister's servant is involved in them and a deal of the fault must lie with themselves.

Feby 28th I must resume now after nearly a week elapsing. I am sore grieved to think that one of the most promising of my scholars – a nice girl of ten years – is seized with that terrible disease the "Lock-jaw", which works such havock amongst the St. Kildians. On Thursday last she was unable to read as usual in school in the forenoon. I thought it was merely her throat that was sore, for so I was told. She returned not in the afternoon and now her life is quite despaired of. What she suffered since Friday is terrible to think upon. She is affected exactly the same as the infants who are seized with it. The muscles of the body appear to be in a state of lasting rigidity, while at the end of every three or four minutes paroxysms of spasm occur, followed by intervals of comparative ease and a desire to sleep till she is suddenly aroused by the excruciating pain which attends the paroxysms.

She cannot rest in the same position five minutes; but must be turned from side to side, or kept sitting or standing. She takes a little gruel occasionally. The mind is quite entire. The following incident appears to me very striking. I had a great liking for the poor girl and she is much pleased whenever I go in to see her. This afternoon after school I went to see her and on entering the room I sat at the foot of the bed without going in her sight at all and enquired in a low voice which she could not hear, how she was. I was not in three minutes when she said to those that were beside her that she was feeling the schoolmaster's breath and asked if he was in. I satisfied her by going beside her. It struck us all as very singular.

O the dear child; she often asks if I am yet come and when sitting in the room out of her sight she as often asks if I went away yet. May God bless you, you dear lamb. How we desire that she would be restored to us in health and strength again; but not our will but Thine be done, O God, for thou doest all things well. O Jesus, cleanse her soul in thy blood. O Holy Spirit give her thy comfort.

March 5th (Saturday) That girl is still lingering on in a state of great pain and is a wonder to all. Every limb and part of her body is affected.

LADY GRANGE CLEIT · ST KILDA

Her very toes are bent downwards. To add to her affliction there is a stoppage in her bowels for more than a week and medicine she cannot take, her throat being so much closed. I offered to give her an injection; but the people are so very curious that they will have their own way do what you will, and what aggravates me still more is that they give her a sort of gruel or paste of flour meal instead of oatmeal. I remonstrated; but to no purpose. She speaks to me every time I go in and today she said she is not worse. Last night and today again they expected that she breathed her last in one of the fits that came upon her. May God bless her.

Beautiful weather since March came in. Oystercatchers came last week.

There is much sickness amongst the people at present. On Thursday last the 3rd inst. I visited most of the people and the following is a list of the sick that night.

House.

Big House [He means the Factor's house] *Mrs. McKinlay swollen and sore feet.*

Big House Ewen Gillies sore foot.

No. 1	*Christina McKinnon sore breast & costive.*
No. 2	*Finlay McQeen sore head.*
No. "	*John McDonald sore eyes and pain in head.*
No. "	*Mrs. M. McDonald eruption on back of neck.*
No. 4	*Neil Ferguson pain in side.*
No. 6	*Mrs. Angus Gillies mind partly deranged. Cannot sleep.*
No. 7	*Rory Gillies Rheumatism in legs.*
No. 8	*John McDonald (blind) pain in head.*
No. 11	*Annie Ferguson: Lockjaw.*
No. 12	*Norman Gillies pain in head.*
No. 16	*Mrs. McDonald rheumatism in whole body.*

In an old house Rachel McRimmon: sore head.

March 10th Up till yesterday we had beautiful weather, warm & mild as summer, for the last ten days. Today snowing all day with bitterly cold wind from the East.

Annie Ferguson, after much suffering since this day fortnight, departed this life about 3pm. today.

Since Saturday (5th) last nothing entered her mouth except cold water, as much as would stick to the spoon at a time and occasionally a drop of wine. It was to us nothing less than a great wonder how she stood it so long under pain that is indescribable. So great had been the pain that the body was entirely out of shape. What a warning to all of us! This day fortnight she was in school with us and tonight the body and the soul are separated. May God bless this visitation of his providence to us all and especially to the young. Why did He spare us and cut her down? I hope and trust she is gone to a "better land" where pain and death never come.

I am much put out to hear that there is one of the boys taken ill and fears are to-night entertained that he is taken with the same trouble as he complains of his neck and jaws.

12th March (Saturday) To-day at 4pm, amidst a heavy snowfall, Annie Ferguson aged 10 ½ years was buried in the part of the churchyard close to the gate. On the part of the women there was loud weeping and wailing and no wonder for from amongst them there was suddenly snatched away a quiet, inoffensive and very obedient girl. Their weeping at the grave reminds me of "Rachel weeping for her children and will not be comforted for they are not."

O Lord bless unto us all this stroke. The dispensation of thy providence may seem dark to us in culling such a fair and promising flower in the spring of youth; but thou art all wise. May it be blessed to her mother who hither has led a very loose life. She was not married; but had this girl to the husband of another woman.

Mar. 16th Snow continued to fall frequently on Sabbath and Monday. Very cold. Wind N.E.

Today is milder with the snow disappearing but the wind is still keeping N.E. Have no school this week owing to the death of the girl. So I spend a deal of my time in walking about endeavouring to gain my wonted appetite for food, from which, with every disturbance and trouble that was in the place for some time back, I had considerably fallen away.

The boy about whom fears were entertained is recovering, nor is it now thought that it was the Lockjaw at all. In other two months we will be looking out for the vessel. How I long to hear from home! I trust in God they are well.

Mar. 21st Fine dry warm weather for nearly the last week. Last week other two of the scholars, two girls, took ill with their jaws neck & pain between the two shoulders, also a little girl under school age. They are all improving but still confined to bed. There are some people in the village – they are few – who must have the blame laid on me in some shape or other. First it was said that the scholars got cold in the Church after going from the Big-house where we were all winter. Mrs. Campbell had them all the winter in the Church and they were two years younger then than they are now and besides the winter & spring was cold & stormy besides what it was with me. Yet they were in no wise affected by the cold. Saturday last I heard that it was a fever that was brought amongst them by my opening a box to give them prizes at Xmas. I opened no box. The prizes came last summer in a parcel which was opened at that same time. There are some curious people amongst them and little heed may be given to what they say; but it is very annoying to have everything cast upon oneself.

Men still weaving. Ten guillemots caught on Saturday. They came about the 8th Inst. and the shearwater about the 3rd Inst.

If I love the fulmars, my most favourite bird in the entire world is the little storm petrel. These tiny dark sooty birds, about the size of a house martin, would come ashore on the island to nest in the walls and cleits nearest the sea in the village area. When I first went out to the island in the late nineties there were two distinct areas of habitation; Carn Mór on the sheer cliffs of the south west was the domain of the larger Leaches petrel and the Manx shearwaters, while the village area was the domain of the smaller storm petrels. Latterly, we know that many Leaches petrels have now migrated down to the village area, as was borne out by a petrel study by Will Miles, a birdie who came out for a few years to conduct a detailed survey on these birds.

The wee 'stormies' are the smallest sea bird in the Atlantic. They breed in the Northern Atlantic and migrate to the Southern Atlantic each winter. They were a source of legend amongst sailors as they will often follow boats. Early sailors believed that they were the souls of sailors lost at sea and a Dutch sailor once told me that in his language they were called 'Feéen Vogel' (fairy birds) and were always a source of wonder when they landed on the decks.

When Will was with us in the summer, Morag MacDonald the nurse and I would present ourselves at the feather store, (Will's headquarters) as he was setting up his fine mist capture nets and activating the recorded petrel call to draw them in. This was usually after midnight and the sound of their call was a loud purring churring noise. There was always a cake or other goodies from the cookhouse, or a gift of chocolate from Morag for Will.

Petrels caught in the nets were carefully disentangled by Will, put into a cloth collecting bag and taken back to his 'office' in the feather store where they were measured, weighed and checked to see if they were breeding and then a numbered ring would be fitted to their tiny leg. Our job was to release them back into the night. Sometimes, as Will handed the collecting bag to us he'd say, 'be very careful with that one' and we'd know that it was a female with an egg. He told us that female stormies can hold onto their eggs for a few days before they decide to lay them, so we always took the greatest of care with those.

Morag and I would take it in turns to take the precious bags out to the cliff edge. I would feel carefully in the bag for the bird, which would (usually) obligingly hop onto my palm, its little webbed feet scrabbling for a purchase. I'd gently lift it out and extend my hand outwards towards the sea and the wee thing would take off out over the water. Sometimes they would sit for a bit getting their bearings, sniffing the night air before launching themselves out over the cliff.

One memorable night, I was on my own and it was the most exquisitely beautiful June evening, warm and still with the waves whispering on the rocks below. The moon had come up over the Dun and a golden shimmering path of moonlight stretched out over the bay. It was after two in the morning and daybreak was not far off. Will had gone out to take down the nets and I had the bag containing the last petrel to release. It hopped onto my hand and I held it out seaward. It sat there looking around, stood up, then sat down again shuffling round, nibbling on my fingers. He looked at me and I at him and then just as I thought he was going to settle down for the night, with a shrug of wings he took off straight along the golden path over the sea. It was such a beautiful moment I was moved to tears. Will, coming up behind me, said 'I saw that one go Maureen, how lovely that was.' A moment like that was worth all the exhaustion I felt the next day from lack of sleep.

When Will left, he presented me with a collecting bag permeated with their unique scent. It's a slightly sharp metallic musty scent not easily described, but one sniff and you know its petrel! He also gave me a tiny feather in a little plastic phial. The smell of petrel when I unscrew the top is still very strong from such a small thing. Whenever I unwrap my collecting bag from its plastic outer bags, it smells extremely strong ... wonderful ... and I am immediately transported back to the island and petrels.

28th Up till yesterday the weather was wet and cold. Today mild &
calm. Men about finished with weaving. Last Wednesday night Malcolm
McDonald Jr. was found in bed speechless about 10pm. and remained so
till about 3.30am. He was in church in the evening (Wednesday) and

was not heard to complain. The nature of the disease was peculiar, nor was he expected to recover. His jaws were closed, his fingers and hands so stiff that they could not be bent, and his body greatly pained. He is now greatly recovered.

April 2nd Weaving finished a few days ago. Women fulling the cloth. Weather good.

In the 1840s the Earl of Dunmore, proprietor of Harris, asked local weavers to copy in tweed his wife's family pattern (Murray tartan) for the purpose of outfitting the workers on their estate. Lady Dunmore was so pleased with the results, she began to market this product and as a result of her enthusiasm, the sale and trade in this type of cloth was soon established; the beginnings of the Harris Tweed industry.

Weaving was the men's work in the winter. They also traditionally were the tailors on the island. The women's work was to card and spin the wool ready for the commencement of the weaving. The bales of cloth produced went towards payment of their rents.

When a length of tweed is removed from the loom, it has a rough, stiff, uneven feel. The women would 'finish' the cloth by softening and shrinking the fabric. The tweed would be washed and while still wet, beaten and pulled by hand on a rough wooden table until it shrank to a specific width and length. The women would sit on opposite sides of the table all pounding and pulling the cloth in rhythm. It was usually accompanied by a traditional 'waulking song' (a work song) which kept the rhythm going. This could go on for many hours.

One wonders how they managed out on St Kilda as Mr MacKay had banned all singing other than psalms and hymns and was responsible it seems, for a general stamping out of most of the traditional social activities, such as dancing and the like, which might be perceived as being in league with Satan, within the narrow confines of his own personal religious zeal and fervour.

April 6ᵗʰ Very cold weather. Hills white yesterday. Ewen Gillies is beginning his rows again. When the "Hebridean" was here he bought some tobacco from Captn. McCallum in the manse and gave it to the minister's servant to keep for him. He now says that some of the tobacco was taken off the roll and a piece of inferior quality put on while in the manse. He is really a troublesome man.

Yesterday the minister commenced catechising the people taking five families at a time to the Church. Out of these families only six came to be catechised, four of them being scholars.

I am greatly surprised that they do not attach more importance to catechising here. There must be some reason this year. There were three girls out of those families fulling cloth all day. I considered it far from being right.

April 9ᵗʰ On Thursday 7ᵗʰ I went with the men to Boreray to kill Gannets through the night. We arrived across sometime before dark. When the night began to fall seven went on land & five remained in the boat to cruise round the island to pick up the birds when thrown over the rocks. D.M., W.M. & I went together and had rare work of it. They (the Gannets) lie sleeping on the ledges of rocks which to any man but a St. Kildian would be quite inaccessible. There is usually on each ledge a sentinel which thinks that he may refresh himself by a short nap occasionally. When he does so the party must pounce upon them, take a hold of as many as possible by the neck and keep them from making a noise lest those in the neighbourhood be scared away, and it was strictly enjoined upon me that though one should take the half of the finger off me I must not make the least noise. They are powerful birds and their long powerful bills are like razors. It is merciless slaughter; but as it is one of the means of sustenance in St. Kilda it must be performed and so you must pocket mercy for the night. Being full moon it was much too clear for making what they call good work. I did not complain of the clearness at all as I could, in places where no cat could get, see where I was going. It is very dangerous work on a dark night.

After working for an hour or two, we rested and had family worship. The scene to me was very impressive. The three of us sat down on the bare rocks with the ropes about our middles, the cloudless sky our canopy, the moon our lamp, and the ocean still and quiet far below, and offered praise and prayer to Him who was able to preserve us in such dangerous work, D.M. leading. In the morning the whole company had worship together on the way home in the boat, D.F. leading. How we should thank Thee O God for the way thou didst preserve us in the midst of such dangers.

Today we went in the morning to kill shearwaters. I had not seen any of these birds previously and, being rather a rare bird owing to the difficulty experienced in finding them, I wished to get one or two for stuffing. So I joined the company and had a hard days work. These birds are to be found in holes far in beneath the ground or below stones. The dogs get the smell of the birds and by scraping make it known in what holes they are. We got about sixty only – very few for two men's work all day. Saw a great many young lambs amongst the Soa sheep, of different colours, yellow, brown, white & speckled.

12th Apr. Mrs. Ewen Gillies of a son Sabbath 10th.

Beautiful weather. Men went to Boreray again last night. I am thankful to God that I did not go, as Mrs. McKinlay, who stays with me, turned very ill about ten o'clock. I did not expect she would see this day. She is certainly drawing near her latter end and has little concern about what is before her. May the Holy Spirit awaken her to see that out of Christ there is no safety.

April 18th A long continuance of beautiful weather. Slight rain last night followed by a stiff breeze to-day.

Died yesterday at midday the child, that was born a week ago, of lockjaw, after a very short illness, being seized by the disease on Friday. It was not baptised as its parents absented themselves from church for several months back.

Mrs. McKinlay still ill and confined to bed. Very troublesome as she won't allow anyone to attend upon her except two women & myself day & night. Her mind is not at all settled.

No school for the last week.

25ᵗʰ Fine weather up till Saturday evening, when it turned cold. Showers of snow yesterday. Very stormy last night. Hills quite white today. Still (morning) snowing. A bad day for lambs.

May 2ⁿᵈ Thou art welcome back again, O Summer. 'Tis thou that I waited for to loose my chains and bid me go free from prison.

Beautiful weather since middle of last week. People commenced planting the potatoes on Thursday. According to custom they all commenced at the same time. Today they commence the oats. Pretty late I should think. At the end of a fortnight now or three weeks at the furthest, we will be looking for the vessel.

5ᵗʰ No oats sowed till yesterday the 4ᵗʰ. On the afternoon of the 2nd we went to Boreray, Stac Lee and Stac Anarmin for Gannets eggs. It was too early in the season. Got only about fifteen dozen, being 20 eggs per man. It was midnight before we got back and got the boat drawn up.

No school today as they are busy with the sowing. I took a good walk up the hills. Saw the first fulmar's egg this season. I cast many a glance across the ocean but saw no vessel. How I long to see the "Robert's" sails in sight!

May 9ᵗʰ Yesterday (Sabbath) very wet with wind S.W. Oat sowing finished today. First puffin's egg got on Saturday by D. McQeen. Did very little studying of late. Commenced astronomy today.

May 14ᵗʰ Spending my time very idly as I am becoming rather impatient now. After the middle of next week I'll expect the vessel daily. Yesterday

I had a great day getting puffins' eggs in the Dùn with the boys. The men were removing the sheep.

May 21ˢᵗ These days <u>seem</u> long. I long to see thee O "Robert Hadden". Working at mathematics. Revised a deal of algebra this week.

Very stormy these last three days. Snowing frequently. Last night was the stormiest summer night ever I saw. Gale still continues. Peat cutting suspended.

May 28ᵗʰ Lively times at present. On Wednesday 25ᵗʰ we went to Soa for fulmars. Wild stormy sea on the side where they landed. I did not attempt landing as they themselves did so only with difficulty. In the boat I helped to pick the birds; got about 500, & a few eggs (Guillemots and Falcs [sic]).

His writing definitely reads 'Falcs'. In my time, we used to have a few peregrines around in the summer but he has not made any mention of falcons at all until now. I thought he meant fulmars, but he goes on to say that the fulmars were all snared on the nest and the eggs left there, so I'm not at all sure which bird he is referring to; maybe it *was* the peregrine falcon and there were more of them about on the island then. I did think of another predatory bird he might have meant but it was not as widespread then as it is today; the Great Skua or 'Bonxie'. There were quite a few bonxies on St Kilda and in the ten years I was there they seemed to increase in numbers.

Shortly after the first raft of puffins arrived in April, their presence was noted. Someone on the base would remark, 'saw the first bonxie today', and we'd all know THEY HAD ARRIVED, just one or two to begin with, but more each week. They looked malevolent; big, dark and brooding with a wing span of up to four and a half feet. The pairs would set up their nesting territories and although there were none in Village Bay itself, they established themselves over the rest of the island.

During the nesting period, the birds became EXTREMELY territorial and would attack viciously on sight, anyone straying into their chosen district. Walking near any of these territories became fraught, as without warning they would attack, swooping down on the head of the unprotected walker and in many cases drawing blood.

One particular site to beware of was a shallow depression in the ground between Mullach Mór and the slopes of Conachar. This was known as 'dive bomb alley'. Our own method of dealing with them was to poke a stick up just above your head as you walked, which usually gave them pause for thought, but as we were aware of just where their nests were, we tried to avoid direct conflict.

I have come across bonxies on other remote islands, but nowhere have I come across any as viciously aggressive as the ones on St Kilda. One afternoon, out walking in October, when all threat of attack was gone, seeing shadows flickering around me, I looked up to see fifteen or sixteen of them floating above me; adults and young, lazily looking down on me as I walked.

One of the warden's chores out there was to go round all the buildings on the base at first light during the fledging season and collect up any baby 'pufflings', petrels and anything else that had got disorientated by our lights and had landed at the bottom of the walls. They would be put into collecting bags and taken to the Factor's house where they would be housed in boxes in the dark until dusk, when they would be released by throwing them gently off the top of the jetty; out to sea and safety. As this was usually the time when work parties from the National Trust were out doing conservation works, it became a popular pastime to go along and help with 'puffling flinging' of an evening. One never-to-be-forgotten time, the warden asked if she could advertise to all on our notice board on the base, that there would be 'PUFFLING FLINGING TONIGHT OFF THE JETTY AT 9.45pm.' This was fine and various parties trooped down there to see the sight. Unfortunately the warden had obviously been anxious to get them off her hands and, not waiting until it was completely dark and with a flourish, by way of demonstration, threw the first one off the top of the jetty. All watched as it flapped its little wings over the sea … where it was promptly 'bonxed' on by a bonxie and carried off. There were cries of disbelief and shock and the rest of the flinging took place when it was properly dark.

The next day there were none collected (the wee things had obviously taken note), and the warden wrote on our board 'NO PUFFLING FLINGING TONIGHT.' Some time later, we noticed someone had amended the notice to 'NO PUFFLING FLINGING TONIGHT … BIRDS OF PREY NOW FULL!'

The fulmars were all snared on the nest and all the eggs were left in the nests. On Thursday the ewes and lambs were brought to the glen & folded there, where they are milked daily. The lambs are shut in at night, & the ewes are milked early in the morning. There is a fold for each family, and it is the womens' part to herd them all day keeping them separate. I was in school.

Yesterday was a great day. All the wedders all along the north side of the island had to be driven to the Camber. This was accomplished in the same way as sportsmen beat the hills for game. The men and boys were extended along in a line on the hill tops while two or three were driving them up from among the rocks below. What shouting on the part of the men, nor did the dogs, eager for the chase, diminish the noise with their barking. 'There was racing and chasing' on Connagher's Side.

Several times a number of the flock would make a rush back through men, women & dogs and then every one was in full pursuit. Of course I was in the midst of all this excitement. The Camber was reached about two o'clock, when the girls came with our dinner. It being now very stormy with wind & bitterly cold we had to go in parties to nooks in the rocks to partake of something from the hands of the fair sex, who were not less excited over the business than ourselves.

Today the sheep are to be clipped today. I clipped seven yesterday and learned them the way to use the shears. Their shearing instrument is the common knife which of course makes work. One man last year got a pair of shears in a present and on my making use of it yesterday it *became an object of wonder and was called a <u>great invention</u>. There was a crowd of about forty men & women in a circle round about me with eyes full wide with astonishment at the strange operation which the beast was undergoing. Remarks such as the following were made; "O graidh! Na gearr an scornan" (O love don't cut the throat). "Na doir as an ghruan" (Don't take out the liver). While the owner of the beast said it would not stay on that side of the island after hearing such "gliogadich" noise about its ears, meaning the sounding of the shears. All this was very amusing to me and today I expect getting some more sport with them.*

June 6th This is terrible. No vessel yet.

On Thursday 2nd the men went to Boreray to clip the sheep. Got two good days last week. Wet & misty today, they can do nothing. Should the factor come tonight, nothing can be done till they return.

The women commenced storing away the peats on Friday, putting them into <u>claets</u> [sic] *(stone huts) on the hill.*

June 11th This is almost beyond endurance.

Last night the cry was got up that the vessel was come. The place was all in a stir, but no vessel came. It must have been a fishing vessel passing in the direction that the "Robert Hadden" used to come. Today the boat is to go to Boreray for the men. They signalled last night that they were finished. This they do by cutting up a large square plot of ground so as to be seen black. Boreray is seven or eight miles [actually closer to four or five miles] *distant ...*

As with the North Uist diary this one ends abruptly. True to his word he has noted on a separate page at the back of his account a list of some of the people who were sick on the island and their ailments. They are reproduced overleaf in full as he wrote them down.

Nov. 14th	*Rachel McRimmon*	*severe pain in head with disordered stomach*
" "	*Alex Ferguson*	*pain in head. No appetite for food.*
" 16	*Christine McKinnon*	*pain in bowels*
" "	*Mrs McDonald (amhuin mhor)*	*pain inside, little sleep last night*
" 20	*Mrs Angus Gillies*	*pain in head*
" "	*Neil Ferguson*	*heavy cough & trouble inside*
" 22	*Norman M. McQeen*	*fainted, afterward great heat in body*
" 23	*Rachel McRimmon*	*pain in head*
" "	*Malcolm McDonald (senior)*	*cough & trouble internally*
" 27	*Catherine McDonald (C. Òg)*	*sore breast*
Decr 9	*Christina McKinnon*	*sore feet*
" 11	*Rachel McKinnon*	*sore head*
" "	*John McDonald (Blind)*	*pain in head & inside* [?unclear]

We know from other documents that it was at least a few more weeks until he successfully made his escape from what had become, as he says in his own words, a prison. The joy over the vessel's arrival and even the knowledge that he had another ten days of the Factor's business with the islanders to go through, before he was bound for home, would not have diminished this elation. His last diary entry sounds extremely anguished and the longing for the vessel that was to take him away all consuming.

Sometimes waiting for the helicopter to take <u>us</u> away after a hard month's tour of duty, felt similar, although to a lesser extent. Although I loved the island in all its aspects, there were times, and that applied to all the personnel out there, when it was definitely time to get away for a while.

My schedule of work out on St Kilda was generally a twelve hour day for twenty-eight days. After landing on the island, I would have a brief chat to the outgoing chef, who would have left me my handover notes in the office, plus the lunch all ready to cook when I got to the cookhouse. Sometimes, if the chopper had been delayed for some reason in Benbecula and it was getting close to lunch time, I would have to run from the helipad all the way up to the base, dash into my room, divest myself of my survival suit, get into my chef's gear and gallop on down the corridor to get lunch cooked before everyone started banging hungrily on the door at 12.30pm. Sometimes the kitchen assistant would have slid the soup onto the stove for me, turned on the steamer for the veg and switched on the oven for the baked potatoes ... sometimes not!

The unwritten rules for chefs out there were that on handover day the outgoing chef had all paperwork up to date, handover notes completed and lunch prepared and ready to cook. He would also have prepared the whole of dinner for the evening, ready in the fridges to pull out and cook. This, in theory, gave the incoming chef time in the afternoon to get their baggage up to their room and unpacked, bed made and personal locker opened. The outgoing chef would also have cleaned, tidied and hoovered the room before leaving.

There were occasional glitches in the system, sometimes due to another helicopter flight coming out loaded with rations. These had to be checked and put away and if time was tight, it was a case of straight into the freezers with the frozen goods, into the fridges with the fresh and the rest left in a heap on the storeroom floor, all to be dealt with after lunch. It was not unusual for me to be making my bed up at 9 o'clock at night and unpacking essentials, having not got there during the day.

Working twelve hour shifts single handedly for twenty eight consecutive days, without much time off, especially if numbers were high due to extra contractors arriving, left me totally exhausted at the end of my month. On the Sunday before the crew change helicopter on the Tuesday, personnel going home would be watching the weather carefully. If it didn't look good, general gloom and nervousness would set in. We found the BBC weather forecasts the most accurate. If it was good everyone relaxed. Fog, mist and high winds, especially northerlies … and things got tense.

On the Tuesday morning, it was all baggage to the weigh-in scales at 8.30am. Personnel leaving were also weighed as there was a limit to what the helicopter could carry and oh, the embarrassment of having put on a few extra pounds over the month! The helicopter safety video was watched by all outgoing in the Puffinn and then it was back to work to wait!

If it was foggy, we'd watch to see if the mist rose up above the quarry on the hill, which meant that the mist was above 500 feet and it was safe for the chopper to come in. The wind … well … we had two windsocks in the bay at different points as some winds produced a lot of turbulence, cross winds and the feared Katabatic winds which would slam you and the helicopter straight down into the sea. There was also the dreaded 'F' word. This was Forty knots and the helicopter definitely would not be coming in if that was forecast!

ST.KILDA WREN
VILLAGE BAY 2008

The pilots we had to transport us back and forth were brilliant. One particularly so, having flown just about everything there is with wings. He was a very experienced pilot and we knew if *he* was coming for us he would usually manage to get in to the island. The pilots had to be extremely experienced, as they themselves acknowledged that St Kilda was not good for approaches and landings. One of the coastguard pilots I also talked to said he would groan when on a stormy night, he was told he was Kilda bound. We were all sitting at lunch once with one of the pilots and he was telling us about a new pilot who had just started on the run. We of course wanted to know all about him, what experience did he have etc. and I remember him reassuring us, saying, 'Och he'll be fine once he's had his "Kilda fright" coming in to land, yep once he's had that he'll be fine.' There was a silence round the table as everyone was fervently hoping that they were not on board while he was having it!

We would wait anxiously and were not surprised when someone would either phone the kitchen or poke their head in the door to tell us the flight had been 'binned' for the day and the pilot was heading back to Kyle and his base. We got on with our work philosophically and prepared for a re-run the next day and so on until we did get off. The longest I have had to wait to get off was ten days. This meant the other chef was waiting around on the Benbecula side while I still had to work on St Kilda, all the time conscious that it was eating into my leave off the island and the time I would have at home in South Uist.

There was also the subject of rations running low, but we always had plenty of stores. If we ran out of fresh milk, there was always dried, which everyone moaned about but accepted as just part of island life. Fresh fruit and vegetables ran out from time to time, but we had freezers and tins and no one went hungry.

It is easy to imagine that the store of food ran out or was running low during George's time out there in 1887 and that is why the birds' arrival back to the island in the spring was so important in terms of fresh food. It must have been particularly welcome; that and the warmer days and longer hours of daylight.

It was interesting for me to note that even in modern times on St Kilda, really nothing much had changed in terms of everyday life on the island. There were still the odd rows, the waiting for the means of deliverance (in this case the helicopter) etc., but there is now a major change on the medical front.

A nurse is in residence at all times. There are three of them, based in Benbecula, rotating shifts of two weeks at a time and covering any medical emergencies out on St Kilda. They are trained in the use of a defibrillator machine and ECG monitoring; they carry out normal surgery routines and procedures, and are trained to prescribe drugs and other medication if necessary. There is also access to the Coastguard for any major emergency evacuations and occasionally in the middle of the night we'd wake to hear the distinctive sound of the coastguard helicopter arrive and take off, finding out in the morning who'd been taken to hospital in Stornoway. This was certainly not an option during George's time and many people died from a variety of injuries and illness, including burst appendixes and the like. There was just no one to help.

I feel so privileged to have worked for the last ten years out on St Kilda. There were good times and bad, but that was the nature of the island. We are indebted to George for the information in his diary ... rows and all, as it gives us a clear insight into a very special island community; one that was wholly dependant on vessels reaching its shores. It is certainly very very different now; there is the internet for global access and good phone links, but it is still there; still the same little group of islands far out in the Atlantic. Still sought by tourists as a destination to 'bag' and boast about having been there. Still with a certain mystic charm when you step ashore. It is utterly unique in the Western world. Life is indeed easier for the 'islanders' that are out there now, but it remains ... as ever ... St Kilda.

THE ISLANDS BOOK TRUST –
high quality books on island themes in English and Gaelic

The Islands Book Trust are a charity committed to furthering understanding and appreciation of the history and culture of Scottish islands in their wider Celtic and Nordic context. We do this through publishing books, organising talks and conferences, visits, radio broadcasts, research and education on island themes. For details of membership of the Book Trust, which will keep you in touch with all our publications and other activities, see www.theislandsbooktrust.com, phone 01851 880737, or visit Ravenspoint at the address below where a full selection of our books is available.

Our publications include substantial conference volumes on island themes such as St Kilda, Alexander Carmichael, Whaling, Emigration, and the School of Scottish Studies; and books in English and Gaelic by leading scholars and writers such as Donald Meek and James Hunter.

The Islands Book Trust, Ravenspoint, Kershader, South Lochs, Isle of Lewis, HS2 9QA (01851 880737)

A SMALL SELECTION OF OTHER TITLES FROM THE ISLANDS BOOK TRUST

See *www.theislandsbooktrust.com* for a full list of our publications

History of Skye	A new edition of the classic book by Alexander Nicolson, edited by Cailean Maclean
From the Low Tide of the Sea to the Highest Mountain Top	A history of community ownership of land in the Highlands and Islands by Jim Hunter with photographs by Cailean Maclean
Alexander Macdonald – Bard of the Gaelic Enlightenment	Edited by Camille Dressler and Dòmhnall Uilleam Stiùbhart
Tiree – War among the Barley and Brine	By Mike Hughes and John Holliday. A snapshot of Tiree during the Second World War when there was a high presence of personnel based on the island
Destination St Kilda – From Oban to Skye and the Outer Hebrides	By Mark Butterworth, including 67 rarely seen original magic lantern slides from the 1880s from the collection by Aberdeen photographers George Washington Wilson and Norman Macleod
Stroma – The Island in the Stream	By Roddy Ritchie, Alistair Murray and George Gunn, including 71 beautiful images of Stroma

Foula – The Time of my Life	By Chris Mylne with over 90 illustrations. A valuable record of island social life in Foula in the 1950s
The Island Lighthouses of Scotland	By John A Love, a biologist and illustrator who has been fascinated by lighthouses ever since visiting the Bass Rock over 50 years ago
The French MacDonald	Edited by Jean-Didier Hache. Based on the journal of a Marshal of Napoleon in the Highlands and Islands of Scotland in 1825
Dualchas àraid agus Prìseil Oighreachd ar Sinnsearan	Two volumes of unique photographs from a collection by Dr Kenneth Robertson, taken from the late 1950s onwards
Exploring the Isles of the West	By Marc Calhoun. Two volumes covering Firth of Clyde to the Small Isles and Skye and Tiree to the Outer Isles
Return to Patagonia	By Greta Mackenzie, following up the best-selling 'Why Patagonia?', tracing many family connections between Lewis and Patagonia from over a century ago
From Cleits to Castles – A St Kildan Looks Back	The autobiography of Calum MacDonald